Dietrich Weiderkehr

BELIEF IN REDEMPTION

*Concepts of Salvation from the New Testament
to the Present Time*

Translated by Jeremy Moiser

John Knox Press
ATLANTA

Library of Congress Cataloging in Publication Data

Wiederkehr, Dietrich.
  Belief in redemption.

  Translation of Glaube an Erlösung.
  Includes bibliographical references.
  1. Salvation—History of doctrines. I. Title.
BT751.2.W4813   1979   234'.09   78-24088
ISBN 0-8042-0476-4

First published in Germany by Verlag Herder KG, Frieburg im Breisgau,
  Germany, 1976

© Verlag Herder KG Frieburg im Breisgau 1976

Published in Great Britain by S.P.C.K., London, 1979

Translation copyright 1979 by The Society for Promoting Christian
Knowledge and John Knox Press

Printed in the United States of America

Atlanta, Georgia 30365

Preface

Discussion of the relationship between theology and reality—of theology's 'relevance'—has usually been prompted by a particular theological question. It must also, however, characterize the whole of theological thought. Of all theological themes, perhaps soteriology has raised the question of relevance most acutely; nor would it be an exaggeration to say that in soteriology the relevance of all theology is at stake. There can be no significant discussion of redemption if man's experience as a threatened being and as a seeker for fulfilment is excluded. Furthermore, the fundamental threats to man and society challenge theology to adopt a positive attitude and to counter those threats with some critical and constructive contribution. Soteriology must see itself, and be seen by others, as just such a contribution; it is not an isolated theme to be studied before or after a succession of other isolated themes; it colours the entire theological spectrum and dictates the direction in which every theological endeavour and discussion—and more importantly all the Church's preaching and pastoral care—must move. The debate on the historical development of Christian belief in redemption, begun some years ago, has thus led theologians to extend their inquiry in ever-increasing circles, and today scarcely one of the formerly isolated themes has been left untouched. If theology does not manage in soteriology to articulate its concerns in such a way that man, with his questions and aspirations, can see himself addressed and understood, then whatever else it may have to say is consigned to irrelevance and unreality. On the other hand, we might hope that an intelligible communication—a positive contribution—here, in the immediate and compelling question of the success or failure of man's existence and of society, can be extended to the whole of Christian belief, theological reflection and the Church's witness.

A critical account of more recent interpretations of Christian belief in redemption must start with a plain statement of fact. Theology has taken a long time, far too long, to realize and integrate into its researches the epochal gap or divide between traditional belief in redemption and man's quest (both explicit and implicit) for salvation today. That gap, unfortunately, has been partly filled by other, non-Christian, movements which have preceded Christianity in their analysis of the ills afflicting man and society and then in the steps they have taken to find effective solutions. Between secularization, with its materialist understanding of human history and social growth, and theology's first attempts to come to grips with the situation through a revision of soteriology lies a large, arid tract in which the traditional doctrine of the fall and of salvation by God through the death of Jesus on the cross has been merely repeated unaltered, without critical self-examination, and in a markedly apologetical and polemical spirit. The result has been that, in the basic soteriological message and in its later interpretation, man's experience of sin and his quest for salvation are determined by quite other considerations. This is not to deny the relevance of earlier soteriological concepts *at the time*, but simply to draw attention to their historical relativity. Now that human history and society, claiming to function according to their own laws and to be responsible to no higher power, have risen up to challenge the transcendent powers of sin and grace, and now that man's potential for the fulfilment or destruction of his life has grown so enormously, soteriology can no longer afford to ignore, in thought, speech, or action, this altered state of affairs.

Scope of the present work

The need for a radical revision of belief in redemption, therefore, arises from the history of ideas and social growth, which we have first to make explicit. In the present work, only a few attempts to supply this need, all of them different in scope and direction, will be described. As with every interpretative event, one author will turn his attention more to the 'text' to be translated and interpreted, yet without departing from his own situation and experience, while another will inquire primarily into that situation and thereby delineate as accurately as possible the direction in which the process of translation and interpretation must move. Our account will attempt to clarify the direction which a revision of soteriology must, in our opinion, follow. First of all, it is apparent that because tradition has scrutinized the biblical sources from determined and circumscribed attitudes of its own and within the range of practical possibilities available to it at the time, it has excluded or at least shown very little concern for the matter of *total* human salvation. With occasional one-sidedness this deficiency has been supplied by recent exegetical work on the Old and the New Testament. For example, scholars are now becoming aware that in traditional belief only the termini of Jesus's historical life, his incarnation and death, have been understood and interpreted as being significant and effective in any true salvific sense. His ministry of preaching and healing has not been considered the appropriate object of *soteriological* inquiry. Again, a radical questioning of the christological tradition of the Early Church, particularly of the great councils, reveals the soteriological relevance—which alone enables us to understand fully the length and intensity of the christological disputes —of the supposedly arid and unreal conciliar definitions. Of all solutions proposed by the Latin tradition of the West, Anselm's concept of satisfaction has been the most prominent; but a radical reinterpretation can discern in it more relevance today than its abbreviated treatment in modern theological textbooks might lead us to suspect. Yet, meticulous though our reworking of traditional themes may be, it cannot entirely close the gap between the modern statement of the question of God and of salvation on the one hand, and all earlier soteriologies on the other. We must therefore concern ourselves also with those new attempts at solution which, usually with a background in the history of soteriological belief, start from man's urgent quest for meaning in an opaque world and an ambiguous history.

The relationship between God and man in guilt and justification—a relationship of which tradition seems often to find little difficulty in speaking—is mainly experienced today in terms of the multiple interhuman relationships of the world as it is experienced. Righteousness 'before God' is withdrawn from the range of man's possible achievements by the demands of society and the iron laws of history. The so-called political factor, even when introduced into theology otherwise than as a critical corrective, concerns soteriology in a special way. The question arises: are we to dismiss all tradition as being incurably privatistic, or are there in fact elements in an earlier stage of theology and the Church which have recognized, and above all practised, the social implications of the salvific event? Even though such precursors would not dispense us from translating our inquiry into the complex structures of modern society, they do offer hermeneutical patterns of how we may ease tension between the original salvific event and witness thereto on the one hand and today's understanding of redemption and salvific or liberating praxis on the other. Of all questions concerning redemption and liberation, that of social utopias is of particular importance. Chief among them is the Marxist theory and praxis of a just society and a reconciled world, so rudely opposed to Christian belief in redemption. In fact this opposition has partly determined the historical development of Marxism. What we may now (with some exceptions) describe as 'polemical dialogue' tended to deteriorate into the proposal of sharply contrasted alternatives: earthly-material or religious-spiritual salvation, social justice or justification by faith, united struggle of the proletariat or grace-filled work of God in Jesus Christ. More recently, the sterility of this approach has been overcome in a dialogue which incorporates critical self-examination, in which each side recognizes in the other common aims (expressed in different terms) of human and social openness and transcendence, and in which, finally, the question of the motives and sources of human liberating action is asked and answered at a much deeper level.

An account of the different modern interpretations of soteriology distinguishes the modern from the traditional approach by extending the range both of questions and of answers. However, comparison with the several more recent articulations of the question of salvation has not only exposed the omissions and weaknesses of traditional soteriology, but has also revealed the potential and the underlying dynamic force of the original biblical witness and of our theological, spiritual, and practical traditions. It has alerted us to their hitherto latent power. The following critical account will therefore be concerned with discovering not only which essential aspects of Christian belief in redemption have been overlooked or truncated and why, but also, and more particularly, how extending the range of questions can help the integral Christian message of redemption to influence and appropriate the Church's belief and praxis.

The present book arose from a seminar which I held at the theological faculty of Lucerne University in the winter and summer terms of the academic year 1974/5. Our basic text was H. Kessler's *Erlösung als Befreiung* (Düsseldorf, 1972). Using that work as point of departure, individual sessions examined the areas of biblical theology, the history of theology, and Marxist theories of emancipation, and so investigated and supplemented the range of sources. In this I was aided by the invaluable co-operation of my colleague Professor Dr Eduard Christen of the same faculty, as well as by the stimulating contributions and inquiries of the students who followed our proceedings with equal scientific zeal and personal involvement.

For the definitive version, my special thanks go to Herr Kurt Koch, Dipl. Theol., Lucerne, whose experience and interest were a source of great help and enlightenment. The bibliography in the notes, on which we co-operated, contains firstly those works with which the present book specifically deals; secondly, those to which I know myself to be particularly indebted in my theological work and in the appraisal of the various currents of thought; and thirdly, those which are added so that the reader may pursue his own inquiries. A complete bibliography is evidently impossible because of the extent of the problem. The aim of the present book is merely to offer a survey and, we should like to hope, some guidelines for judgement.

Lucerne, Easter 1976   DIETRICH WIEDERKEHR

Contents

Conclusion

1

Experiencing and bridging the gap between ourselves and traditional soteriology[1]

The movement from an unarticulated feeling of alienation to its linguistic analysis and then to its theological-historical consideration is a lengthy process. Not all the several phrases of that process lie within the province of scientific theology, but all hearers of the word, and also the theologian himself as their contemporary, are more or less consciously interested in it. The new interpreters of soteriology, naturally dissatisfied with mere feelings, ask why the traditional discussion of fall and salvation, sin and redemption, sounds unfamiliar and has lost its impact. It enumerates the various codeterminative and linguistically formative factors, though at the same time guided by a more or less explicit new feeling and awareness, for the sake of which it is going to remodel traditional attitudes to fall and salvation. If it is to be successful, this undertaking presupposes an equally fundamental analysis of man's new understanding of himself, on the basis of which the exposition of fall and salvation is to be redesigned. Such a process, whereby traditional language is discarded and a new language evolved, can only be described as a movement (that is, as a passage from a *terminus a quo* to a *terminus ad quem*). In theology, critical distance and creaturely quest alternate in importance. A knowledge of both termini of the hermeneutical process is presumed and implicit in all attempts to bridge the hermeneutical gap.

1 From unintelligible to intelligible salvation

Soteriology is indeed the theological area in which we react most sensitively to contemporary ways of expression. No matter how sin and salvation be understood and articulated, every soteriological statement seeks to address and to be understood by the personally-involved subject. Unlike other themes such

1

as the doctrine of God, Christology, and eschatology, the business of soteriology has always been primarily the study of man as the proper subject of fall and salvation. Even before any programmatic anthropocentrism in theology, such as characterizes our own complex of problems, soteriology always envisaged man as the object and recipient of God's salvific activity. Without man, soteriology could never have achieved linguistic formulation. Consequently the history of man's experience of sin and his expectation of salvation, as well as their linguistic expression, affect this theme in ways that are constantly changing.

From this we may conclude, not surprisingly, that when the Church passed from the age of the New Testament to another level of experience and another cultural environment, the language in which the original message of fall and salvation was proclaimed inevitably appeared unfamiliar. It became necessary to seek an idiom that would be relevant and understandable here in the realm of soteriology the need to reshape the notions of biblical theology assumed a degree of importance greater than in any other field of inquiry. At the same time, a need was felt to extend the process to the entire proclamation of faith, because (and only as long as) a detached and isolated proclamation of God, Christ, and the rest of the Christian message was unthinkable. In other words, soteriology was essential for the understanding of God, Christ's Person, the fulfilment of man's earthly history, and so on. The source of this linguistic conflagration, of this all-consuming linguistic fire, was the soteriological terminology affecting man directly. But the impression of alienation and the consequent demand for an idiom that would express the notion of salvation more immediately and intelligibly, more critically and so more helpfully, were inevitable. That much can be said apart from such questions as whether or not the full spectrum of human experience of sin and expectation of salvation was expressed in the various forms used to proclaim salvation, or whether particular aspects were already foreshortened and new horizons excluded. We cannot legitimately, without qualification, reproach biblical soteriology (or for that matter other historical linguistic means of proclaiming salvation) with having excluded essential subject-matter. The reason for this is that the integrity of the spectrum of the experience of fall and salvation cannot be assured merely by articulating modern man's understanding of himself. The new idiom resulting from the hermeneutical process is to be judged from a twofold standpoint. First, does it accord with man's self-understanding, with his articulation of experience, at this particular time? And second, does it disclose and bridge the historical gap between traditional and present-day experience?

2   *Shifts in the soteriological spectrum of experience*[2]

Although we shall not, I hope, succumb to the simplistic and one-sided view which reduces the historical difference between traditional and modern soteriology to the statement or scheme 'transcendent fall/salvation—worldly fall/salvation', even a summary comparison still reveals a shift in the spectrum of experience. This is the basis for our critique of traditional soteriology and for every attempt to find a new interpretation of fall and salvation. An impartial analysis of biblical conclusions and also of tradition continues to reveal in many places a broader spectrum than appears possible to a superficial and simplified knowledge of tradition. Yet the centres of gravity and the crucial elements of the experience of fall and salvation in the Bible and those of today do not coincide. In biblical and in traditional Christian thought man's transcendent relationship to God—a broken and mended relationship—stands in the foreground, whereas for modern man (and the Christian proclaimer and hearer of the word naturally regard themselves as included in this category) the fundamental experience is of this world and of his own historical situation. On the one hand, therefore, tradition includes great systems articulating the contemporary understanding of salvation, starting with the Old and the New Testament; and these systems study among other things man's basic relationship to the manifold structures and experiences of the here-and-now and those of human relationships. On the other hand, most attempts to find a new interpretation start from an all-important self-containedness of the world and argue to a transcendent relationship to God. Despite this basic openness and universality of the experiential spectrum, the respective priority of the transcendent relationship to God and of the experience here and now of salvation affects the total picture. The dominant factor leads all too soon, in less-than-comprehensive presentations and understandings, to a narrowing of the spectrum. Because it is proper to the Christian understanding of salvation (as opposed to a pre-Christian/heathen, immanent conception, or even an excessively materialist conception of salvation within the Church) to describe fall and salvation, in the real sense, in terms of man's relationship to God, this transcendent relationship becomes increasingly dominant, while other aspects, such as man's earthly corporeal needs, social and political slavery, and the dangers threatening man's existence from within history recede or disappear. Conversely, it is hardly surprising that the effort to correct the narrowing of horizons characteristic of traditional soteriology now lays particular emphasis on those neglected aspects; man's transcendent relationship to God and his eternal future gives way to these here-and-now, interhuman, and structural relationships (although this is not to be mistaken for reducing them to the same level). The history of belief and of theology proceeds not by way of agreed syntheses, or at least not always, but in dialectical counter-movements in which neglected and emphasized factors alternate.

3   *Critique of the relative nature of traditional soteriologies*[3]

Like 'political theology', critical reflection on the social implications of belief is a modern phenomenon. It would, on the other hand, be a misrepresentation of the earlier history of belief and of theology to call that history totally apolitical merely because there was no conscious connection between the basic relationship of faith and its social conditions and consequences. Earlier soteriological models, even those that appear to have been strictly religious and transcendent, were subject to a critical analysis according to their social relevance. It is clear that theology has always stood in a mutual relationship with contemporary social conditions, either as their ideological sublimation and sanctioning or as their critical corrective, latent perhaps but discovered sooner or later. Whatever the

4

precise nature of that relationship, the traditional concepts lose any claim to be above time.

This, however, is not only a loss, but also a gain. Being *conditioned by* time means also being *relative to* time. Earlier models attain their intelligibility only in the context of their contemporary historical situation, with its particular cultural, religious, social, and political structures; and it is impossible to break out of and abstract from time. Still, it is such a knowledge of tradition which justifies us in making analogous modern interpretations of fall and salvation. The same insight into the time-conditioned nature of theological, even dogmatic, statements takes on a critical function that sharpens awareness. Although the deficiencies and limitations of earlier soteriological concepts become clearer as we study them, we also learn that we are not ourselves immune from the same sort of blindness in our present situation, and that theology will still be unable to exclude both impoverishing and enriching experiences. There can be no ideal theology superior to reality; theology must accept and welcome in freedom the fact that it is conditioned by time, but it will also be intent on preserving and regaining its freedom.

4   *The divide of secularization*[4]

A new interpretation of soteriological statements cannot, therefore, be either avoided or even deferred, for between tradition as a whole and the modern question of salvation lies the ideological divide of secularization: the understanding of the world, as far as possible, in causally immanent and rational terms and the human self-understanding which strives for autonomy. By far the greatest part of traditional discussion of fall and salvation is governed by an uncritical theonomic interpretation of man, of his history, of his experience of the world. God's claims and man's responsibility before God are therefore understood on this level of ideas: the dependence of the world and history on God for their existence is paralleled by man's responsible relationships to God. The positive or negative nature of this relationship determines, decisively and fundamentally, man's experience of sin and need for salvation. More recently, however, theology has become aware of the

5

deficiency of this presupposition. The ineffectiveness of Christian preaching on repentance and atonement is not simply the result of a regrettable moral weakness on the part of modern man. It arises also from his inability to understand himself as the recipient and subject of a salvific decision, at a time when the theonomic relation of the world and history and of man's dependence on and orientation to God are no longer the presuppositions of his thinking and experience.[5] We may not, indeed must not, conclude from this change that the entire transcendental concept of salvation is to be dismissed lock, stock, and barrel, but at least a new Christian interpretation of the Church's soteriological statements must incorporate this shift of emphasis. A credible and honest understanding of fall and salvation will never wrench a Christian from the ideological companionship of his contemporaries and plunge him back into a pre-critical attitude towards the world and an immature curtailment of his responsibilities. A new interpretation of fall and salvation cannot simply and without more ado insert the transcendental alignment of these experiences into the here-and-now or interhuman relationships, without, that is, a properly differentiated hermeneutic. Nor can it confine fall and salvation to human self-understanding and free self-realization regarded as potentialities independent of any transcendent correlative reality. On the other hand, this transcendent relationship and this transcendent confrontation of man in his existence and freedom cannot be thought of and articulated apart from the structures of intra-world and interhuman reality. Similarly, credal statements of God-wrought salvation must defer to the awareness of freedom characteristic of the modern age.

5   *Reality lost and regained*[6]

Finally, the narrower thematic of soteriology brings us to a problem which concerns fundamental theology, and indeed theology as a whole. Can soteriology become an intelligible and significant discipline relevant to man's total reality? Soteriology is not merely a particular province of theology. It contains a reference to man, to his existence, history, experience of the world, and social ties, all of which must be either formally perceived by soteriology on behalf of theology in general, or lost by soteriology and consequently by the remainder of theology. The person or nature of God, Jesus Christ, the Church, the sacraments, grace, creation, and eschatology cannot be accounted for in a pre- or extra-soteriological exposition the purpose of which would be merely to add some minor aspects of significance to man. No, the content of all theology is to be understood and interpreted *from the start* in a soteriological context; the nature of all theology may be defined as soteriological. To confirm this, we need perhaps make only one observation. Discussion of the relevance of theology, which is often highly abstract, gains in intelligibility and seriousness as soon as we substitute for this formal definition the richer characterization of a soteriologically oriented theology. Does theology speak, and does the Church act, soteriologically or not? The question involves the presence and relevance of theology and of the Church in modern man's experience of the world and of history. If, therefore, even a stunted form of soteriology can make relevant the Church's belief, theology, preaching, and praxis, then the attempt to evolve a newly interpreted soteriology is more than a partial undertaking: it is a proposal ultimately to force all theology out of its isolation until the remotest realities are brought into its purview. Not only is attempt to establish such relevance doomed to abstractness and formality as long as it omits this bias; it would also give rise to every possible misunderstanding of the Church's tutelage or ecclesiocentric control of man. But if this formal relevance of theology is unequivocally expressed and realized as *soteriological*, then the alienated and sceptical person to whom it is addressed will at once have a clearer idea of what a relevant theology might mean to him.

2

A soteriologically guided re-examination of the biblical sources[1]

1   *The basic problem of historical interpretation*

Christian belief always has a twofold theological duty. First, it must take seriously the contemporary form of the question of salvation; but second, it has to answer that question in fidelity to the original salvific event and to Christian understanding of it in the past. The faith must not neglect either of these two poles. It must not simply question, historically, the biblical understanding of salvation without at the same time striving to transpose it into contemporary terms; nor conversely can it simply translate or modernize it without endeavouring to deepen understanding of its historical origins and later development. A reference to the Bible must not be just the selected manipulation of a few theological themes detached from their historical and religious context and used to satisfy a modern expectation or solve a modern problem. On the other hand, it must not reject as time-conditioned, and so as inappropriate to the solution of a modern problem, those aspects of biblical soteriology which at first sight appear to be unsuitable. A hermeneutic of soteriology has to be no less cautious than a hermeneutic of the so-called dogmatic elements of the faith, such as in Christology and ecclesiology. These apparently less practical elements of theology have yet evolved from the standpoint of their soteriological significance, as is shown, for example, by the messianic expectation and the messianic preaching of Jesus.

It is therefore insufficient to extract a few soteriological terms and look for possible parallels or points of contact in modern thought. Any comparison must be between the entire situations in which the question of salvation is posed. Within this wider area individual concepts and methodologies can then be more accurately assessed. Such a comparison will reveal similarities as well as differences; there are human experiences of sin as acute in the past as in the present, although other experiences perhaps have no apparent parallel. But even the similar experiences may have a different source and significance in the New Testament and in the world of today. For example, personal justification through the works of the law can be achieved only with difficulty, while we find man's present concern for freedom in an anonymous society neither expressed nor satisfied in the New Testament as we might have expected. We might formulate the following general judgement. Soteriology as expressed in the Bible sees man's ultimate nature primarily as imperilled, and asks how that nature can be saved. We, on the contrary, try to view man's nature in its past and present historical and social framework, with which we are often too little acquainted. Man's peril and salvation are consequently considered today in social terms, for example as concern for material wellbeing, in unbalanced or successful human relationships, as the improvement and humanization of the social fabric; these levels of concern do not necessarily lead to a transcendent depth in man or in history. This general difference, therefore, forbids us to transpose individual soteriological concepts uncritically from one level to another; it requires us to investigate hermeneutically the common features implicitly present at both levels.

The fact that biblical sources can and should speak to all their readers, of whatever historical period, arises from their peculiar nature; it belongs to the history of their development. The writings of the Old and the New Testament are the documentary deposits of a process of tradition which not only preserves and commemorates decisive original experiences of salvation but also incorporates them into the altered experiences and situations of the contemporary believing community. In this connection we have only to think, for example, of the use of the Exodus tradition in Israel's later historical crises, or of Christian discipleship in the communities of Jewish or gentile Christians. The two periods are often described as quite separate ages of man, the 'biblical' period and that of today, especially when all biblical sources are considered to lie on the far side of the chasm created by secularization. Nevertheless, with the

9

Bible was initiated a process of transmission which is recommenced with every new historical age and will continue in the future. The degree of reflection with which we look back on this process and continue it ourselves has, however, changed and improved.

2 The return to the Old Testament in the Christian study and practice of salvation[2]

Examination of the biblical sources today differs from that employed by traditional soteriology, because the source-area and the horizon of inquiry have both been extended. Christian soteriology was for centuries content to exploit one or two central statements of the New Testament in connection with the salvific event of Jesus's death and resurrection. While a substantial part of his salvific activity and preaching was sacrificed as the horizon narrowed, the Old Testament was also sadly neglected, if not wholly disregarded. Salvation in the Christian view was distinguished mainly by a polemic against the earthly, materialist, political expectation of the Old Testament. At first no one noticed that in this dualistic and evaluative contrast—an imperfect Old Covenant and a perfect New Covenant—even the total salvation preached by Jesus himself was truncated. One would have thought the co-ordination of promise and fulfilment, of historical expectation and realization, to be sufficiently prominent in the Old Testament, but it was overlaid with a qualitative classification which ultimately was thought to culminate in the rejection of Jesus by the Jews. The reason for his rejection was considered to be that he did not fulfil their material and political hopes but sought to lead them to the higher plane of spiritual goodness. The result, on this view, was Jewish unbelief, and finally the rejection of Jesus on the part of Israel. The Jews were said to have failed to recognize and accept the spiritual, inner nature—the transcendence—of the salvation brought by Jesus as the real fulfilment of the Old Law. If there was occasionally an appeal to the Old Testament, it was only by way of confirming and answering a systematic thesis. Neglecting the Old Testament concepts of salvation, biblical theology looked for traces of or testimonies to the transmission of an original sin, justification by the gift of the Holy Spirit, and the gradual emergence of a hope in eternal life. Such questions, however, lay properly on the fringe of Israel's salvific expectation and conception, and these were generally by-passed as of small significance.

The first duty of an original reinterpretation of the message and person of Jesus has been to look again, this time more closely, at the background of the New Testament, and particularly the Old Testament. What Jesus meant by the Kingdom of God, what man was saved from, and what he has been given in the new age of salvation could be learned only from the context of the New Testament; it could not be determined by working backwards from later concepts of salvation which had unduly narrowed the horizon. This has meant that the Old Testament also has become an essential source for Jesus's understanding of salvation, some elements of which coincided while others clashed with the salvific expectation of his listeners. The precise way in which the ideas of Jesus surpassed and differed from the expectations of salvation entertained by others cannot be known unless the content of the accepted concepts and the significance of the accepted symbols in language or action, such as 'gospel' or 'the breaking of bread', are known. The recovery of the historical perspective for an understanding of Jesus has not allowed theology to stop at him, as if he had instituted a completely new terminology and symbolic language for human salvation. It has forced theology to relate Jesus to the history of Israel as to his horizon of experience and expectation.

This historically conditioned examination of the Old Testament has been necessitated also by a simultaneous displacement in the content of the Christian understanding of salvation. Critique of Christian tradition had increasingly concentrated upon that tradition's tendency to spiritualize and situate it in the afterlife, and theology has thus been obliged to consider whether and how the Christian understanding and practice of redemption related to man's bodily and social expectations and fears. Doubt about the justice of a spiritualizing view of salvation could no longer be suppressed. Bonhoeffer,[3] for example, in his programme of 'non-religious interpretation', adduced the Old Testament's expectation of total happiness,

11

which was not to be diverted by promises of eternal life or spiritualized interiority. Thus the *present-day* interest in the neglected aspects of salvation has come to assist the scrutiny of the Old Testament demanded by *exegesis*; this has helped to sharpen, but also to complicate, the inquiry. Not only is there now, for the purpose of clarifying New Testament texts, an exegetical interest in the Old Testament's understanding of salvation; it is also hoped that the Old Testament will enable us to deepen *today's* Christian understanding and practice of redemption. Ultimately it is often impossible to say which of these two interests has been and is the keener in expounding Old Testament soteriological texts and concepts.

Theology is now subject to a grave temptation very similar to that which threatened earlier theologies. Traditional soteriology looked for, and then found, a transcendent and other-worldly salvation, and took its finding to be the witness of Scripture. Similarly defective would be a study of the Old Testament that looked for confirmation of modern forms of salvific hope and salvific realization without including the whole field in which contemporary experience took place and developed. However tempting it may be to regard Israel's liberation from Egypt as the model for social liberation and the attainment of freedom for the oppressed, the analogy contains dissimilarities as well as similarities of experience and understanding. For Israel, the experience of the Exodus was interpreted as part of a covenant mentality, and it must therefore be located within the relationship of choice and obedience between Jahweh and Israel. It must not be seen as an independent human bid for freedom, much less as a first attempt to escape theocratic rule.[4] In this comparison we must not choose isolated concepts and processes, but relate all concepts and processes to their theological background. N. Lohfink, for example, adopts just such a method when he proposes to extend the comparison of mere *words* to the comparison of word-*fields*.[5]

3 Old Testament notions of complete salvation[6]

To harmonize the modern question of salvation and that of the Old Testament is made easier by the fact that the latter does not move on the periphery of human experience and history, much less outside it, but concerns people who call on God to satisfy basic human needs and thank him for granting rudimentary human favours. So, for example, the relationship of the covenant[7] not only includes a strictly 'religious' relationship between Jahweh and Israel, but also extends to the whole spectrum of human experience, whether it be the organization of life or society's relation to the world and nature. God's grace-filled approach is not confined to some invisible arena, but takes concrete shape in the leading of the people and its individual members, embraces the families and the people, and provides them with a country and with essential goods. Israel was to recognize in all those blessings the proof of God's fidelity. At the same time Israel's obedience to the God of the covenant was also extended to include all those areas. The people reciprocated God's choice not only by fulfilling the cultic commandments, but equally by rendering justice to one's neighbour, by showing mercy to the poor and to strangers, and by grateful acceptance and joyful use of life's good things.

The several areas of life were controlled by the law.[8] Increasingly detailed legislation threatened to undermine the law's basic purpose, but at decisive points the law was again placed in the strict context of the covenant and of God's promise to his people. This also fixed the social and political duties of the Israelite in the context of God's election and commandments. The result was that the fulfilment of particular items of the law, even in the extreme ramifications of daily life or right doing, was part of the one indivisible history of the covenant. Where a narrower piety limited itself to observing the prescriptions of cult, the prophets reminded the people of the demands of human justice and love. And then God's blessing and curse, the continuance or rupture of the history of election, were also measured by observance of the commandments. In the course of the transmission of the law, Deuteronomy in particular stressed God's amity towards men and his concern for the poor, for strangers, and for animals and nature; the sabbath, for example, was to benefit them all.

Above all, however, the concept of salvation for the whole man and for all of life was revealed by the eschatological

13

promise[9] of salvation, and for our present purposes it does not matter whether this universal salvation was part of God's direct rule or was mediated by a messianic saviour. The remembrance of an original act of salvation gradually gave way to the expectation of a future redemption of man, of the people, and of the world. The repeated delays and disappointments in the fulfilment of that expectation—the effect of which was to encourage Israel to consider the promised land, the new temple, and the return from exile as provisional fulfilments (and also disappointments) to be superseded in their turn—could not divert the nation from the hope of an ultimate and at the same time universal salvation. Israel did not adopt the obvious (mis-)interpretations of a spiritualized, inner, or uniquely other-worldly salvation. This eschatological universality was not a mere horizon somewhere in the remote distance but shed a critical light on the people's *present* belief and practice. It also, however, provided in cases of need a hope of restoration, justice, and life.

As regards the unfolding and articulation of salvation, the history of Israel affords privileged patterns according to which this experience of salvation was preserved and developed. Thematically, salvation lay in the cultic situations of the prayer for forgiveness, in the cry for help, and the prayer of thanks for favours granted, in the celebration of Jahweh's nearness to Zion, which meant salvation for Israel and also partly for the world. In daily life and in ethico-religious education, salvation was often regarded as a matter of 'do right and you will prosper'. On this understanding, human responsibility and decision gained in significance, while in other contexts salvation was solicited rather as God's free gift. But despite the presence of common features in the Old Testament concept of salvation and the modern question, an important difference must not be overlooked. Even though much emphasis was laid upon man and his conduct, and even though the individual was to over-come injustice and do right in his own personal relationships, salvation was still *God*'s work. Also, God's salvific activity ultimately took place mainly *within* the existing structures of contemporary society; deep-seated change figured in only a few eschatological promises. Again, this highlights a difference between the Old Testament and the modern understanding of salvation.

4 Salvific praxis and preaching of Jesus[10]

It is noticeable that in their treatment of New Testament soteriology scholars are no longer concerned with the two 'classical' poles of interpretation of Jesus's work, namely, Eastern Christology and soteriology on the one hand, which regarded the incarnation as the decisive salvific event, and Western soteriology on the other, which interpreted the death of Jesus almost exclusively as sacrifice and atonement. Both forms of soteriology, moreover adopted a somewhat static approach which did less than justice to the salvific events in the life of Jesus. They saw redemption in the event considered as most important: in the East, incarnation as the assumption and divinization of human nature; in the West, a satisfaction of infinite value in the death on the cross, by virtue of the hypostatic union. It is clear that both views were mainly systematic approaches which, rather than interpreting the soteriological texts of the New Testament, even those relating to the birth and death of Jesus, on the basis of their biblical setting, imposed upon them a different category of thought. Thus whilst in New Testament theology Jesus's birth and his death are situated against the background of his whole life, in traditional soteriology the significance of his life, or that part of it which lay between incarnation and death (or resurrection), was not apparent. The life of Jesus either unfolded the redemption that had already been brought by the incarnation, or merely led up to the all-sufficient sacrifice of his cross. It finally lost any right salvific meaning when a dogmatic system was imposed on the doctrine of the 'mysteries of Jesus's life', still preserved in scholastic theology. That life was treated as a series of models of Christian activity or as a succession of informative, but not symbolic, illustrations of religious salvation. Although a proper study of Jesus's preaching and practice would have yielded a more accurate interpretation of his death, that death would still not have been seen against the background of his liberating praxis during his life before the resurrection; it would still have been part of an independent theology of sacrifice.

15

Later, post-New Testament soteriology, however, was not alone guilty of narrowness in this respect; it was already present in Paul's reduction of the Christ-event to Jesus's death and resurrection, and in the retroactive interpretations of Jesus's life as a journey to the cross. In the end this journey, as a thing significant in its own right, was lost to sight.

The correction of this process, which situated redemption on the fringe of Jesus's life, is one of the aims of Kessler's interpretation of his death.[11] This interpretation seeks to take out and evaluate as independent and autonomous soteriological factors the individual events in the life of Jesus as found in the transmitted units of the synoptic gospels. Kessler does this with such determination that the peculiar implications of the cross are in fact neglected—although one might maintain that this imbalance is justified in the total context of his work. Accordingly, another way of understanding redemption becomes possible. Corresponding to the Christology of the synoptics in its original form (in so far as this can be reconstructed), redemption is no longer the result of one self-sufficient meritorious act on the part of Jesus; his person, preaching, and praxis are all placed in a theocentric context. The God from and for whom Jesus acts, preaches, and lives is not, however, an abstract being, but the concrete subject of the eschatological event of the Kingdom. This Kingdom is the background of all Jesus's activity, message, and claims, as well as of his specifically salvific discourses or effectively salvific actions. This approaching horizon of the God who comes in power and benignity fills the particular deeds and encounters of Jesus with a presence of salvation; we no longer need to look to other events in his life, whether earlier or later. Thus, for example, his meeting with the blind man at Bethsaida (Mark 8.22–6), the healing of the man possessed (Mark 5.1–20), and the meal with tax-collectors and sinners (Mark 2.15–17) are eschatological salvific events in their own right: the presence of *God*'s forgiving love and healing power is given concrete form in the words and deeds of Jesus, and is received by these people. Simultaneously with this strong reference back to God in his dawning Kingdom, Jesus's person and praxis move, on this view, beyond themselves to other men encountered in particular situations. Jesus

16

receives as it were strong anthropocentric impulse from his theo- or patricentric mission, in so far as his person in this Christological scheme does not draw attention to itself but confronts the actors in individual soteriological situations with the reality of God's salvation. In this context the only possible form of Christology is one already soteriological, one that cannot be divided up into a revelation of Jesus's person on the one hand and a separate revelation of his work on the other. We shall have occasion later to return to this 'implicit' Christology.

Here, however, we have still to establish the variety and breadth of the soteriological spectrum which results from Jesus's openness to the human situations into which he introduces his eschatological claim and power. One would properly have to enumerate all those needy individuals whom Jesus encounters as he goes on his way. They would include those hearers of the good news who are no longer shouldered to one side as illiterate; those who share in the joy of Jesus's table, tax-collectors and prostitutes rescued from ostracism, and also those to whom Jesus manifests his healing and helping power as signs of God's coming Kingdom, even though it may be impossible, in any particular account of such a miracle, to distinguish between historical witness and interpretation.[12] One thing should be clear from these signs of total human salvation: with God's coming, man is finally rescued from his partial existence and restored to total life, integrity, sight, and hearing.

Moreover, this healing activity of Jesus is accompanied by a definite eschatological index of time. Not only does the person of Jesus reveal another urgent demand for repentance and an already habitual readiness on God's part graciously to forgive, to save, and to liberate. Both now receive an urgency and an added depth. For once there is no suggestion that they are to be surpassed in their turn; Jesus addresses to his hearers a call to repentance that cannot be deferred and in which their own entire future is at stake. This urgent call, however, is only the urgency of God's gracious nearness drawing people and nations to himself. In Jesus, God's Kingdom comes in a way that speaks to the inmost heart of man, whom God accepts once for all as his own. The expulsion of demons through the power of God is only the obverse of God's liberating advent (Matt. 12.27).

17

Even more important are the social implications of God's Kingdom. The dismantling of existing differences and barriers between learned and simple, just and sinners, is not simply the revolutionary programme of Jesus and his social freedom; it results from the unconditional love of God, who now turns to all men. As the previous division and discrimination against sinners, tax-collectors and the uneducated derived from an ideology that claimed that it alone enjoyed God's discriminative love, so this social component now belongs inseparably to the proclamation and fulfilment of God's eschatological love. There is now no way of reaching God's love other than in Jesus's companionship with tax-collectors and sinners, in his healing of outcast lepers, in his teaching of people neglected by the scribes. The parables, which in the synoptics are interwoven with his activity, bring out the latter's theological and christological relevance (cf. Luke 15.1–10). Conversely, Jesus's activity gives the parables a solidity that raises them above the level of mere illustration and imagery.[13]

5 *Praxis of Jesus: prototype or source?*[14]

Two other relevant questions have been repeatedly asked in the history of Christian belief and of understanding of the redemption. What meaning does this dual relationship of Jesus to God and man give to his own person; and to what extent is his activity more than an exemplar which is, of course, pre-eminent and initiatory but which can and should be copied more or less adequately by his disciples and by believers in general?

These questions arise from a standpoint which concentrates on those to whom the gospel is addressed and their various situations, and which draws on them in order to understand the exemplary and binding force of Jesus's conduct. We cannot be fobbed off with the traditional view that Jesus acted as the Messiah and his activity was primarily a gospel that not only imposed legal obligations, but also opened the way to discipleship. An exact analysis of the scriptural data shows not only that the Bible repeats these questions, but also that new answers are included which are more strongly linked with the concrete situation and so give greater concreteness both to the Christo-

18

logical and to the soteriological answer which cannot be separated from it. When both our questions can be answered from a common base, a common understanding of Jesus's person and praxis will also become possible and assist our lives as believers. This is the principal context chosen by Kessler as the starting-point of his soteriology.[15]

The question of Jesus's person is posed by his preaching and practice. The claims he made and his authoritative activity, which do not exclude opposition to the law and tradition, lead us to ask what is the source of his authority, who did he claim to be? In the earliest phase of Christological speculation we find no explicit answer to this question in the form of titles or similar attributions, but a pre-titular account of the person of Jesus which must be explained from the context. Above all, his activity reveals a relationship between Jesus and God which exceeds the communion with God characteristic of the pious man or the prophet's awareness of mission. Jesus derives his own activity from God's activity, not merely in the sense that he sees in it the model of human activity in general or knows he is especially bound by God's will. He understands himself, his preaching, and his activity in close connection with God's eschatological nearness in his Kingdom. The passage to this ultimate hour cannot be deduced from extraordinary natural or historical phenomena, but is revealed in Jesus's demeanour, in the fact that he now preaches and 'practises' the gospel of God's Kingdom. Conversely, Jesus does not point to an event independent of his own person. Rather he encounters man as the personal materialization and historical making-present of God's Kingdom. Jesus does not always explicitly state this identification, but it is the necessary conclusion from his 'definitive activity'. It is seen for example in the linguistic parallel which names in the same sentence God's Kingdom and Jesus's own person: 'If it is by the Spirit of God that I cast out demons, then the kingdom of God has come upon you' (Matt. 12.28). Yet Jesus reveals a relation between himself and God which does not weaken the force of his claim and authority but which discloses that relation as something original and unique.

In and from Jesus the background of divine origin receives

19

a new and underivable definiteness, which is not constructed from pre-given images and names of God, but is filled out and defined by his actual behaviour. This latter must be seen as an interpretation if we are to understand rightly the significance of Jesus's reference to God as his Father. Even though both before and after Jesus all men were encouraged to call God 'Father'; even though the title has Old Testament precedents and Jesus later allowed his disciples the same form of address, he enjoys in this respect a priority not derived from previous usage and an originality not matched in the extension of the right to others. Jesus understands and realizes God's Kingdom in this new and original manner of address: against the formerly hidden, now revealed, and yet still mysterious background of 'the Father'. This underivable and unique relationship raises the person of Jesus above the just men and prophets who preceded him; nor can the disciples, who are invited and called to a relationship with the Father, be placed on a level with him.

It is important to see how this distinctive relationship of Jesus to the Father is made apparent, not in isolated words and events, but whenever Jesus directs to another person his claim and the proof of his love. His own soteriological praxis and his eschatological claim are inseparable from this relationship to God. Even before that activity is defined and denoted by the particular significance of *Jesus*, it is known by him and by those whom he addresses as the experience of *God*'s nearness. The novelty of Jesus's person results primarily from the novelty of the experience of God, and even in subsequent ages it must remain within this larger context in order to be properly understood. Isolated systems of Christology and soteriology touching the person of Jesus were no part of New Testament belief and cannot be so for us today.[16]

Hence it is also clear why Jesus offers his own activity as an example to his disciples and hearers, and so inaugurates a new way of seeing and acting; and at the same time any fear that this will reduce his behaviour to the level of *mere* example[17] is seen to be unfounded. Thus it is not enough for man to accept God's love and be liberated into a new relationship with God and the neighbour; he must at all times *do* what he is *given*.

20

The nearness and dawning presence of God's Kingdom must be visible in man's own behaviour, just as the question of Jesus's authority is posed not merely by himself, but also, in the early community, by the relation of his disciples to the law and the sabbath: 'Why do your disciples transgress the tradition of the elders?' (Matt. 15.2; Mark 2.24; 7.5). The transmission of Jesus's new line of conduct becomes thematic not only in the demonstrative parable of the unmerciful servant (Matt. 18.23–35): 'I forgave you all that debt because you besought me; and should not you have had mercy on your fellow servant?' (vv. 32–3). The disciples too consider existing barriers between groups, social and religious classes, as no longer valid. In Luke's version the reproach is no longer aimed directly at Jesus but at the disciples, that is, at the community which is to appropriate and put into practice Jesus's behaviour, his motivation also and his power: 'Why do *you* eat and drink with tax-collectors and sinners?' (Luke 5.30). Christians could apply to themselves the legitimation Jesus conferred on himself. His person remains present in the 'you' or 'we' of the disciples and the Church, who possess no foundation for their new way of life except Jesus himself. His exemplary demeanour does not simply rank the disciples' praxis *next to* his own; it leaves them in a relation of origin which can never reach the same absoluteness and originality. Even when the disciples act like Jesus, they always do so by his power and for his sake. While they are brought into the new relationship of God's children, Jesus addresses them always from his more basic relationship to the Father. Quite soon the title of Son[18] was seen to be the only adequate expression of his uniqueness.

3

Death and resurrection of Jesus as a salvific event[1]

The New Testament and later theological tradition regard the death and resurrection of Jesus as central to the doctrine of salvation and its theological reflection, so that a special chapter devoted to that event is appropriate. The new interpretation, however, has disengaged itself from a tradition which for centuries dominated not only piety and a simple understanding of the faith, but also theology and liturgy.

1   *Situating the death of Jesus in the context of his life*[2]

In the past, theologians tended to reduce soteriology to the theology of the cross. Such an approach was both inadequate and unhistorical. The New Testament itself, however, is guilty in this respect. Paul's emphasis on the cross leads him to neglect the earthly life of Jesus, and the synoptic gospels have been described as 'histories of the passion with long introductions'. When the total life-history of Jesus was obscured—in early Christology by the use of ontic categories, in medieval soteriology by a strongly juridical theology of satisfaction—the salvific event was viewed as consisting in one of two crucial events: the incarnation (Eastern Christology) or the death (Western soteriology). Theologians became more and more blind to the context in which the historical event of Jesus's execution—and its theological interpretation in the primitive community's understanding of itself—could be properly situated. The salvific significance of his death was finally located in an isolated will-to-self-sacrifice and in a death detached from the life-history. The significance of the violent death remained intelligible for just so long as the Church continued to attach validity to such concepts as expiation, satisfaction, and sacrifice. Such concepts no longer enjoy their former value; the significance of Calvary must now be derived from the larger context of Jesus's whole life and work.

22

Furthermore, in interpreting the death of Jesus there is the wider problem of the relation between the Christ of faith and the Jesus of history. Just as any post-Easter interpretation of Jesus's person and history must ask what support it has in his own self-understanding if it is not to mythologize and endow with meaning an otherwise meaningless person, so the strongly developed theological interpretation of Jesus's death in the New Testament asks how he himself went to meet that death, how he understood and achieved it. Without such inquiry and a positive reply, any subsequent attribution of salvific significance would be altogether groundless.

The answer to those questions can be reconstructed with fair probability from the historically ascertainable reactions, both favourable and unfavourable, to the preaching and praxis of Jesus. He aroused the opposition that finally brought about his death, not by an explicit messianic claim or even by the assumption of a divine title, but by his liberal attitude towards legal tradition. His salvific mission and God's manifest will were always for him more authoritative than tradition. Jesus infringed the law not in a spirit of arbitrary or irresponsible freedom, but with a freedom that knew itself subject rather to God's will than to ancient legal formulae which were no longer applicable to the contemporary human situation. Jesus's persistence in this liberal praxis, its accompanying interpretation in his authoritative preaching, and the advent of the Kingdom of God must have made his death more and more likely and increasingly less of a surprise to his contemporaries. The motive behind his conduct, which jeopardized his continuing survival, was therefore the reason why he risked and ultimately suffered death. On the grounds both of a theological interpretation and of the inner motivation of his behaviour, we may say that Jesus suffered and accepted death in obedience to the Father's mission and out of an invincible salvific love for man. That love did not come into existence at the moment of his death; it was already embodied in his life. The continuity in the mission and obedience of Jesus means that his death arose, one might almost say, naturally out of his life, that the existential experience of death and its free acceptance was not simply a concluding phase tacked on to a qualitatively different existence. Although it has been primarily a question of realizing that the death of Jesus cannot be isolated from his previous life, that it lay in strict continuity with that life and was of a piece with it, Calvary must not be reduced to a fringe situation. The various theological interpretations of the salvific significance of Jesus's death, which often start from an isolated consideration thereof, cannot simply be dismissed as superfluous; they can retain their proper significance in the context of a theology that gives due weight to his life.

2 *Stunting of the soteriological interpretation*[3]

Biblical, and in part medieval, soteriology could look for the salvific significance of Jesus's death by drawing on available and intelligible categories of interpretation without attempting to justify them on every occasion. In the intellectual climate of the New Testament, concepts such as representation, sacrifice, expiatory suffering and death, the suffering of the just man, ransom, redeemer (in Hebrew, *goel*) were still familiar from Old Testament tradition and prophetic and cultic literature, and had already been developed in the Old Testament in spiritural, personal, and ethical contexts. Jesus himself, the bearers of the Jesus tradition, and the theological forces of the primitive community (for example, Paul) moved, like their readers and listeners, within the same conceptual world. Those key-words sufficed which had come gradually to be accepted and which evoked without difficulty in the minds of contemporary listeners a wealth of implicit traditions and concepts. In the words of institution at the Last Supper the concise terminology used made possible an admirably compact theological statement. Their very conciseness, in fact, made further clarification necessary later on. It was evidently sufficient for the primitive community to construct the significance of the words at the consecration of the bread and chalice out of such pregnant phrases as 'body for you'. 'blood of the covenant', and 'shed for many'. As long as the corresponding anthropology (for example, 'body' and 'blood') were familiar to those who heard them as members of a community celebrating the eucharistic liturgy, they were understood as denoting more than elements of a human being; the entire corporeal, earthly reality of man was designated as 'body', his God-given, continually responsible life as 'blood'. Similarly, it was superfluous to introduce the person and life of Jesus, even his passion, expressly into the context of solidarity and community. As well as the salvific significance of Jesus's death as representative, the short phrase 'for you' also recalled his status as God's obedient servant and the entire context of the old covenant. The concise formulas and the inherent system of reference made a personal understanding of Jesus's death and its far-reaching salvific significance easily accessible.

As can be imagined, however, those short formulas are misleading when we no longer presume and appeal to their original setting, when the preaching of Jesus and the eucharistic liturgy have ceased to take place in the context of Semitic-Old Testament anthropology, when they no longer possess a living and intelligible relationship to the Old Testament and its theological categories. In these circumstances the listener will try to find meaning by reading into the words 'body' and 'blood' a significance derived from his own anthropology. But those terms are no longer synonymous with the whole human person. They stand for the elements out of which the person is made: the static 'flesh' and the flowing 'blood'. Whereas cultic concepts such as 'expiatory sacrifice', which were derived from legal language, were raised far above their original level in Old Testament theology by the prophets' critique of cult, outside this immediate area and horizon of understanding the categories had to achieve an independent significance derived from elsewhere, for example from a strongly legal or mercantile concept of God. Because they must be explained somehow, the terms are filled out with a conceptual content which agrees little or even not at all with the original content. The problems of isolated consecration and the associated theory of concomitance could arise only because 'body' and 'blood' were no longer understood as denoting the whole man. A similar regrettable shift can be discerned between the biblical theology of expiatory sacrifice, personalized in the suffering of the just man, and Anselm of Canterbury's theology of satisfaction derived from his construing of the New Testament. This interpretation is due to the fact that religious concepts conditioned by the environment in which they arose were used to fill out the vacuum left by interpretations which were no longer understood and which really signified a relapse into a magic relationship to God; for example, only human suffering or the painful loss of life could obtain the favour of the gods.

3 *Exposition of the soteriological interpretation in the context of human experience*[4]

The problem posed by the salvific significance of Jesus's *death* could be seen as a problem only when an age of natural and ontological thought had given way to one of historical thought. As long as the salvific significance of the particular acts of Jesus's life was based directly on the dogmatic foundation of the hypostatic union and the corresponding infinite merit of the human acts of the humanity of Jesus united with the person of the Logos, the principal difficulty was to clarify the necessity and pre-eminence of his obedience to self-sacrifice and death. For that, however, there sufficed reasons of convenience (*convenientia*) which stressed the special transparency and force of the passion before God and for men. Theology came nearer the biblical understanding of death when it began to regard human existence not as a timeless and constant entity but as the sum of a freely planned life in which death affords an outlet for the unavoidable and radical experience of human finitude, and presents that finitude to man as the possibility of his decision. Death is thus not merely the temporal end of a series composed of particular free situations. Towards it and from it those situations together make up the whole of human life. Man can bring the unfree ending of life by death to a free completion through an existence which confronts and accepts death. He gathers up in one gesture the fragments of all his individual decisions, each one provisional and mutable. This condensation of life may, but does not necessarily, coincide with the moment of death; but only the acceptance of the experience of death gives validity to an anticipatory moulding of life's potentialities.[5]

Various forms of such an anthropological explanation of death have been tried. Their common feature is the mutual influence exercised by life in its fullest extension and the closing hour of death. They differ in situating man's radical decision and his free disposal of the whole of life's potentialities. From the passive experience of death which is at the same time an active free acceptance of death, attempts to pinpoint man's act of total decision move in two directions: forward towards a decision of man already confronted with his transcendent ground at a moment beyond death, or backward into the continuing process of life in the course of which man tries to survey his life as a whole, grasp it, and bring it to a culminating expression of his freedom.

In either case we can give fresh significance to the condensed biblical formulas of Jesus's redeeming dying and death. Even though biblical and modern existentialist ideas of man are hardly coterminous, they coincide in so far as they explain man's life not only as the unfolding of an underlying nature but as the historical experience of his creaturely finitude.

4 *Jesus's experience of death and of God*[6]

The interpretation of Jesus's death in terms of human experience and life-history also clarifies the theological aspect of this experience. The recent orientation of dogmatic Christology to New Testament Christology has highlighted not only the movement and development of Jesus's life on earth but also, as part of it, his relation to God. This latter, by virtue of an exclusively ontological conception, had remained enclosed for centuries in the divine nature of the incarnate Logos. If the unity of Jesus with God is seen primarily in his unique relation to God and its experiential shape, real insights are achieved into his life and experience of death. While acceptance of a static 'divine nature' and its union with human nature makes it difficult to accept a genuine human history, a relationally structured Christology offers the possibility in Jesus of a genuine history of belief and experience. The Christology of the synoptics, no less than Paul's interpretation of death of Jesus, reveals just such a history. We have only to think of the different forms of the words from the cross in the synoptics, ranging from abandonment by God (Mark 15.34) to trustful self-commitment to the Father (Luke 23.46), as well as Paul's understanding of Jesus's

27

death as an example of perfect obedience (Phil. 2.8). The relation between God and Jesus is made clear for all to see in different forms of experience which emphasize now the communication and participation of divine power, now distance and the denial of ultimate self-mastery. In the synoptic pericopes Jesus experiences God as the one who has sent him and given him authority, but also as the withdrawn source and hidden future of his life and freedom. If this dialectic can exist within the life-history, in the frontier situation of death it reaches an intensity possible only there. This context is also chosen by the new soteriology when it comes to the true salvific significance of Jesus's death. The experience of death presents a trial of faith in which Jesus is placed before the hidden and withdrawn future of his authority and life, and endures that hiddenness. At the same time he submits to the Father's will and love without grasping at security in this trusting belief. The salvific significance of this free fulfilment of death becomes even clearer when, precisely in this acceptance of death, Jesus numbers himself along with all men in their relation to God. This solidarity with man is expressed, for example, in the typology of the first and second Adam (Rom. 5.18f); today it is also posited with reference to man's broken experience of God. In his turn, Jesus shared the universal doom of death imposed on mankind in consequence not only of an 'original sin' in the remote past, but also of every disobedient and unbelieving man's own sinful selfishness. From Jesus's free and believing experience of death, on the other hand, arises a redemption which breaks open that selfishness, at least in the sense of destroying its uncertain darkness. Jesus carries his belief and obedience to the point of death; but if death means the ultimate solidarity with humanity in humanity's believing and unbelieving history of sin and salvation, then the death of Jesus begins a turning-point in history which radically alters the relation of all men to God, not only in the hour of death but even in their lifetime.

This critical and at the same time initiatory experience of death on the part of Jesus has not only made possible a more credible interpretation of his unity with God; it has also reached an area of the mystery of Christ that was regarded traditionally as being at the furthest pole from the experience of death, namely the trinitarian relation between Jesus and God as a relation of Father and Son in a unity of life pertinent to the history of salvation and ultimately to God's inner life. It has taken theologians some time to root the divine life of the Trinity in the relationship to God characteristic of Jesus's ministry and of man's Spirit-given sonship of God. At first the 'visionary' hours of Jesus's relation to God seemed to offer a more genuine insight and more practical access into the trinitarian mystery of God's life. But the unity of both forms of the Trinity ('immanent' and 'transcendent') needed to prove its validity in the extreme crisis of death and in the definitive affirmation of resurrection through God. Yet as the expression of an experience of the absence of God, of abandonment by God, Jesus's cry on the cross refers to his origin from God and to his reference to God; the abandonment is mortal because the unity had previously, during the life of Jesus, constituted the all-embracing background of his life. When later the resurrection of the crucified Jesus was understood as an act of God's power and the Father's faithfulness, the negative question of death, which cast doubt on Jesus's unity with God and his election by the Father (Matt. 27.43)—which were claimed by Jesus and exercised in authority—was answered. From this basis in experience the otherwise abstract concepts of intra-trinitarian distinction and unity achieve concrete form unthinkable in a doctrine of the Trinity restricted to God's 'inner' life. In God's communication of life at the resurrection, the nature of God's inner life becomes clearer; and in the hiddenness of God and in Jesus's abandonment in death, the nature of the distinction of persons in God also becomes clearer.

The fourth gospel provides systematic soteriology with a more useful foundation than does the Christology found elsewhere in the New Testament, because it is based on the idea of sonship. Using richly condensed phrases, it also understands Jesus's death and glorification as a 'departure to the Father' (13.1), a 'lifting up' (12.32), a 'glorification' (12.28). Drawing on this insight, H. U. von Balthasar has presented the *mysterium paschale*, in a consistently trinitarian way, as the culmination of the Son's sacrificial mission and as the definitive communication of life from Father to Son. Among Protestant writers, J. Moltmann unites the theology of the cross and the doctrine of the Trinity by presenting the death of Jesus as an 'event between God and God'. Such an event is seen in its fullest implications only within this relationship, not elsewhere outside it or below it. Thus the theology of the cross has shown Calvary to be the point of intersection of two otherwise remote areas of God's being and reality. In the death of Jesus, the life of the Trinity was opened to all men, whom he represented and with whom he identified himself by dying, even in the godlessness of sin and sin-wrought death. Conversely, the whole situation and history of man's sin became the history proper not of Jesus alone but of God himself, and was therefore made accessible to God's eternal love. Even though there is the danger of a consistent systematization in this superimposition and interpenetration of God's being and human becoming (for example, in the shape of the apocatastasis or eternal conquest and abolition of sin and judgement in a still more victorious salvation), the risk is justifiable because otherwise we should not be doing justice to the paradoxical commentary on the cross found in the New Testament: 'Christ redeemed us from the curse of the law, having become a curse for us—for it is written, "Cursed be every one who hangs on a tree"—that in Christ Jesus the blessing of Abraham might come upon the Gentiles, that we might receive the promise of the Spirit through faith' (Gal. 3.13f).

5   *The cross as a legitimate or ideological means
    whereby meaning is conferred on suffering*[9]

Apart from the ultimate unintelligibility of the New Testament's soteriological content, its revision has become essential for the reason that the same unawareness of progressively constricting interpretation and hermeneutical terminology has entailed a further danger. The earlier interpretations we have already mentioned—'redemption through death', 'purification through blood', etc.—are the result of a hermeneutical effort which tried to wrench meaning from the initially meaningless and absurd event of Jesus's death. The individual stages of this effort still reveal how the early community came only slowly to accept a paradox of history and a divine will they could

30

not grasp. The passage from 'was it not necessary?' (Luke 24.26), through 'let the scriptures be fulfilled' (Mark 14.49), to the significance of Jesus's death based on the idea of ransom (Mark 10.45) was a long one. The attribution of meaning to the death of Jesus was achieved only with great effort, particularly as the guilt seemingly entailed by his rejection and the scandal of the cross could be neither approved nor extenuated. The danger, however, was near. And it is also clear that *bestowing* meaning *on* the cross by appealing to God's salvific activity, Jesus's own intentions, and the salvific efficacy of Calvary came unconsciously to be mistaken for an inner *possession* of meaning *by* the passion and cross, even by the death itself. The meaning originally conferred on this event *from without*, despite inherent meaninglessness and absurdity, could later be misunderstood and misconstrued as a mysterious *internal* meaning. Further, the more developed soteriological interpretations increased this tendency by obscuring the inner meaninglessness of the cross. They were used to betray their original purpose by becoming a principal, expanded legitimation of the passion and death. On the analogy of this hidden and later revealed significance, man's suffering was seen to be a sharing in the suffering and death of Jesus, and thus a sharing in Calvary's mysterious salvific significance: the *particular* significance of his suffering became the *general* inner significance of suffering as a whole. Present criticisms of and doubts concerning the new soteriological interpretation are to be understood, consequently, against the background of this dubious history of the theology of the cross. The modern critique of religion has seized on the doubtful use and misuse of the idea of the cross wherever the shorthand formula 'cross' (with its inherent salvific significance) was used to justify existing suffering and the toleration of eradicable injustice. When the critical analysis of causes and the possibility of conquering pain matured, this theology of the cross was seen to be a regrettable obex: it described as 'mystery' what was in fact human injustice; it admonished people to suffer even where individuals and society possessed the means of alleviating poverty. Theology furnished a 'reconciliation of God with misery', which made theology into the accomplice of the powerful and the oppressor and denounced any effort to achieve liberty as disobedience[10] to God's will and a denial of the cross.

Consideration of the death of Jesus as an integral part of his life and healing work has proved to be a soteriology critical of ideology. The actual road to the cross and the theological motivation of the historical Jesus have been more pronounced than in stunted and independent soteriological interpretations.

It was precisely Jesus's longing for man's salvation that drove him, for example, to heal on the sabbath without waiting for the first day of the week. The resulting conflict with the law and its guardians led to increasing opposition and ultimately to violent resistance to Jesus. If therefore the cross followed from Jesus's consistent salvific work, it should not have been cited later as an example of patience and toleration of suffering. It is the abiding sign of the determination of God and of Jesus to free men as individuals and the human race as a whole in all its manifestations. The fact that Jesus's ministry apparently miscarried and led to his death, and that God himself drew life from it at the moment of its greatest failure, should not be regarded as sufficient to establish an unalterable law of human history. One may not argue, from the fact that God did not allow the ministry of Jesus to terminate in death but led him out of death, that this sort of life must necessarily be brought to a similarly apparent impasse, or even left in one.

It is no surprise that this fatal history of effect, which should rather be called a history of non-effect, has made the approach of soteriology cautious and wary with regard to traditional soteriological interpretations. These latter are compromised by their improper arguments and the misunderstanding that results. A soteriological system that takes into account the social situation and resolves not to ignore the critique of religion must choose another, less trodden path.

6 *Prototypal significance of the resurrection of Jesus*[11]

Although medieval theology considered the salvific significance of the mysteries of Jesus's life before Calvary and gave some attention to his ministry (though much less than to the detailed interpretation of his death), that ministry and its salvific significance were increasingly neglected by the schoolmen. Such

32

neglect notwithstanding, a comprehensive theology of Jesus's death, for example in the doctrine of satisfaction, ought still to have given some account of the epistemological foundation of its own arguments. Only from the viewpoint of Easter may one speak of the salvific significance of the cross; without the resurrection the mere fact of the cross would not have been worth transmitting to posterity. Even though it did not establish the real, inner salvific significance of the resurrection, by recognizing that no theological and soteriological interpretation of Jesus's death was possible except from the viewpoint of Easter, that significance would have emerged at least within the doctrine of redemption. But in this way the interpretations of Jesus's death, even in this direction—as was the case with his preceding ministry—achieved only a significance immanent in the cross.

The resurrection of Jesus, however, has attained its unique salvific significance only in the context of and in conjunction with a revised form of eschatology. The connection between the neglect of the resurrection in traditional Christology and the objectification characteristic of traditional eschatology is paralleled by that between the present association and reciprocal illumination of the two themes, which are now seen to be in effect one. In a developed eschatological perspective, the resurrection has assumed new significance both as the real anticipation of the *eschaton* and as its exemplary and efficient cause. Conversely, the resurrection of Jesus has bestowed on the scattered fragments of eschatological discourse a coherence which has enabled statements on a variety of different levels to be co-ordinated and reinterpreted. A genuine demythologization has resulted from this centring of eschatology upon Christology. The view that regards the resurrection as an anticipation of the ultimate end—however the latter may relate to and exceed apocalyptic conceptions—has led in recent years to a concentration on salvific praxis. The distinction and the separation in time, found in scholastic theology and gradually introduced into the consciousness of believers, between Jesus's resurrection and the 'resurrection of the dead' can no longer mean the postponement of an active and effective salvation. At least as regards the ethical sphere of individual conduct, this consequence is explicitly stated in the New Testament's Christology and beliefs concerning man: 'We were buried with him by baptism into death, so that as Christ was raised from the dead by the glory of the Father, we too might walk in newness of life' (Rom. 6.4). The new life of Christians in the Spirit should also affect their life together and their intercourse with the world. All this has encouraged Christians to draw out the social implications of the newness of life and attempt to dismantle the social structures that embody sin and lovelessness. Ethical obligation and spiritual effectiveness are no longer to be limited to the individual sphere, but are to be extended in a theological and practical hermeneutic to the interplay of individual and society.

The anticipation of post-resurrection existence in present activity has been not only imposed by the central truths of the Christian faith, but also favoured by eschatology's reassessment of goals pertaining to the world and history. In other words, a new outlook has been imposed from within, while critics of religion have accused Christianity of inactive otherworldliness; and these accusations, supported by the active hopes of Christians themselves, in whose minds it was to inaugurate the promised world of the resurrection within history, have corroborated it from without. But unlike the external pressure from the historical and social situation, the internal pressure exerted by this understanding of Jesus's resurrection gives rise to an impulse which an already realized eschatological reality possesses over all eschatological postulates.

The fact that a theoretical and practical concentration on the future characteristic of modern ideologies and a reshaping of disjointed Christian eschatology have coincided in time must not prevent us from making a critical distinction. The resurrection of Christ cannot be advanced simply as a concrete illustrative model, a particular historical example, of the universal and necessary truth of a future-oriented history. No, it is the only corrective of all other eschatological horizons. This can also be seen in soteriology, which has been greatly influenced by the general eschatological tendency. Above all, the unbreakable link between Jesus's death and his resurrection has proved to be a discriminating and novel criterion of eschatological tendencies. As a temporary reaction from the previously one-sided view of Calvary, theologians evolved a similarly one-sided theology and soteriology of resurrection. Now, however, the intensely negative preliminary to the resurrection—namely, his death—has forced itself on the attention of theologians and obliged them to modify even the most optimistic syntheses of soteriology and eschatology. What is the real source of this new view of man and the world? 'Death' stands symbolically for those people and those historical situations which of themselves contain no present or future potentialities, and to which all future within the world and history is denied. As the one resurrected *from the dead*, however, Jesus makes his own this situation of man in all its forms. Only the future *he* opened is valid as the universal future, because it alone is tied to and conditioned by no presuppositions ('works of the law'). It is, on the contrary, unlike all other eschatological utopias, addressed and open to all, and cannot be limited by any negation, relative or absolute, not even that of human impotence, guilt, and death. The future newly opened by the resurrection has its sole source at the heart of this absolute negation of the future. It obliges and enables Christians to perceive and confront every negativity of man and history in the light of a real and possible hope.

Resurrection from the dead thus extends from the particular reality of Christ's resurrection. to a perspective of hope which reveals and opens the future of all individual and social forms of death. Deeper concentration on the event of Jesus's death and resurrection has thus helped eschatological soteriology to find its *proprium christianum*.

4

A critical analysis
and reinterpretation of
soteriological tradition[1]

In attempts to adopt a critical attitude, the urge to reinterpret
soteriology often starts from tradition. Even when the purpose
is to interpret redemption as gift and demand in the context
of contemporary thought and practical needs, the exegete does
well to direct his inquiry to the paradigms laid down by history.
This, of course, is not to say that he is limited to them. Critics
of the faith and scholastic theology often lack a basic, first-hand
knowledge of tradition. Simplified concepts and categories are
proposed and rejected as 'tradition' without due regard to their
different provenance. Some recent soteriological studies, while
making the right critical approach to tradition, evaluating
earlier attempts from the point of view of their presuppositions
and potentialities, and acknowledging their defects, have
become increasingly aware that their predecessors in this field
occasionally forecast but failed to grasp firmly and develop the
most advanced theories and objectives of modern soteriology.
For our present purposes, some traditional lines of thought may
be briefly outlined and analysed. We shall see that they
anticipate modern problems, and that four historical forms of
soteriology recover their significance for us today. These are
primitive Christology, Anselm of Canterbury's theory of satisfaction, the Anabaptists (a marginal current of the Reformation), and Religious Socialism. These traditions have again
shown that movements of the past are properly understood only
when taken in conjunction with their history of effects.

1   *The soteriological implications of primitive Christology*[2]

Apart from the remoteness of its naturalistic and ontological
categories, the main criticism of primitive Christology—a
Christology embodied in the dogmas and tradition of the

Church—is that it had no soteriological content. It spoke of Christ in terms of his inner person, neglecting any relationship to man. The preference for biblical Christology and the evolution of a new interpretation of the mystery of Christ's person has been guided by precisely this concern to span the fatal gap between Christology and soteriology with a Christology that is soteriologically relevant in itself. The New Testament predicates are now preferred for their functional significance to the metaphysical predicates of dogma, and the precedence of the *pro nobis* in reformed theology was not only implicit in its methodology, but also logically maintained. This led to a greater relevance for the contemporary question of salvation, but also apparently away from dogmatic tradition. If, in the much-quoted words of Melanchthon, the *beneficia Christi* were more important than those *naturae*, the resulting Christology depended increasingly on the horizon and categories dominating the philosophy and society of the time.

A closer inspection of the context in which the traditional isolated dogmatic formulas had their source has led us to correct the prejudice according to which the theology and belief of the primitive Church were concerned solely with the refinement of a speculative gnosis at the expense of the inseparable question of salvation. The conceptual disputes were not merely the result of a love of speculation; they were motivated by a genuine concern for salvation belief.

The formula referring to divine homoousia is seen in a new light when it is taken in the context of the Eastern Church's experience of sin and expectation of salvation. For the Eastern Church, man's plight consisted in his loss of knowledge of God and in his consequent need for re-education. The latter was imparted to him by the divine Logos, whom Clement of Alexandria and Irenaeus, for example, situated in the context of this human expectation of salvation. This understanding of salvation as a *paideia*, however, was happily coupled with the theory of divinization. Education brought not only knowledge and the better life, but also a refashioning of man in the divine image. The way of redemption was not reduced to moral re-education, but was raised to the level of a transformation of man. Associating the theory of redemption as pedagogy with

37

that of redemption as communication in God provided a healthy corrective of both theories. The divine pedagogy achieved a more vital fulness, while the communication of divine life was linked with the need for personal decision and saved from being misunderstood as a naturalistic redemption which could have resulted in a dangerous blurring of the chasm between God and his creatures. In short, the synthesis of disparate categories of redemption could avoid the defects inherent in each one singly. It was therefore vitally necessary for the Church to defend the homoousia of the revealer and divine model against the heretical attemps of Arius to undermine it.

The history of dogma soon experienced a similar need to defend the integral humanity of Christ, which had been slurred over in the zealous maintenance of his divine consubstantiality and of an inner unity in Christ and in man. This was soon revealed as a latent misunderstanding in orthodox anti-Arian Christology. Arius had, in order to assert the highest possible degree of unity in Christ, substituted in the man Jesus the divine nous for the semi-divine Logos; but on the other hand the orthodox Christology of Athanasius prevented the human soul of Jesus from achieving significant ontological and soteriological stature. The underlying fear was that recognition of a rational free soul in Christ might exaggerate the possibility of sinful freedom. The massive unity-formulas of Alexandrian Christology and the concomitant uncertainty as to what exactly was meant by *mia physis* (one nature) created confusion and obscurity. The model used by Antiochene Christology offered a better critical approach in this respect. It refrained from proposing so strong an ontological unity in Christ on the basis of a more radical distinction between God's infinity and man's finitude. It preferred to tread a path on which it derived the ultimate unity of the divine Logos with the man Jesus from a grace-filled indwelling and self-communication on the part of the Logos, and conversely enabled the man Jesus to enjoy unity in radical openness and surrender to God. Naturally, this unity now included freedom without its being disqualified as simply 'moral' unity. (This had been the objection against Nestorius, inevitably on the Alexandrian concept.) This Antiochene Christology gave rise to an equally urgent soteriological interest in Christ's integral humanity. How could our humanity be redeemed in him if he had not accepted it in solidarity; if, above all, Christ's human reason and freedom were supplanted and absorbed by the ontologically united Logos? 'What Christ did not assume has not been redeemed', so ran the new cry. The ontological content of belief in Christ was not divorced from its soteriological implications. Human knowledge and freedom need salvation most because they are the prime subjects of ignorance and sin.

This context enables us today to form a more balanced judgement and gives us a new understanding of primitive Christology and its dogmatic formulation. Nevertheless, this soteriological context answers only one question while correctly posing another: does not this nexus, it asked, relativize dogmatic tradition in so far as the primitive Church's experience of sin and expectation of salvation were based on only one of many horizons of understanding and expectation? Even though these christological predicates turn out conditionally, against all expectation, to be functional, what significance can they retain for us outside this conditioning context? This question, which every soteriological interpretation of Christ's person and life must ask itself, will recur several times in the following pages. Answering it is ultimately the problem of fundamental theology, whose business it is to reflect on and control any contemporary attempt to situate belief in historical contexts of understanding.

2 Anselm of Canterbury's theory of satisfaction[3]

This particular soteriological theory, which dominated the Middle Ages and later theological tradition, clearly demands a critical scrutiny which examines it in its original, unsimplified form and makes a proper assessment of its defects and omissions. Anselm's soteriological idea considerably influenced the Christology of such great scholastics as Thomas Aquinas who drew on it for the decisive motive of the incarnation. If man's infinite guilt, he argued, was not to be merely overlooked in God's mercy but actually removed, there had to be a satisfaction which only a human subject of divine, infinite worth could make (S.T., III, 1, 2). He also suggested (ibid.) other motives for the incarnation which later scholasticism tended to ignore. This soteriological theory has been more and more adversely criticized in recent years. Its juridical categories dramatize the relation between God and man in an almost commercial way. The predominant demand for God's justice introduces distorting, idolatrous features into our concepts of God. And finally, here again the salvific event is concentrated on the death of Jesus, his life and ministry being regarded only as preparation for and preliminary to the expiatory sacrifice. Such criticism, however, suggests that its proponents are concerned with a simplified and incomplete version of Anselm's theory.

In a study of the theory as originally presented, G. Greshake, among others, has remarked on the many accounts of it which coarsen, simplify, and so betray Anselm's original intention. The polemical value of Anselm's theory lies in the fact that it tries, not to establish satisfaction as the *a priori* motive and indispensable condition of the incarnation and cross, but to understand the reasons (*rationes necessariae*) for the witness and fact of faith. Consequently the foundation of justice almost exclusively developed 'from below' must be differentiated from Anselm's earlier foundation in God's mercy. It is an act of divine mercy to open up for man reconciliation in justice. However, the most important contribution of Anselm's teaching lies in the fact that it presents the relationship between God and man in guilt and reconciliation as one of freedom and obedience. The usual term 'juridicism' is in this respect very wide of the mark. We must rather contrast Anselm's theory with the Eastern doctrine of redemption, which, especially in its later form, made the salvific event very much akin to a natural process. Anselm's theology is part and parcel of Western tradition, the categories of which, though predominantly juridical, did incorporate the human person and his freedom. It also inaugurated a christological development which thought of Christ more 'from below', that is, placed him beside man over against God. Nevertheless, the same soteriology also introduced a momentous gulf between Christ's so-called objective work of redemption and the so-called subjective acceptance of redemption by man. Christ remains ultimately on the side of the grace he merited without entering constitutively into the relation of believing and redeemed man to God. 'The grace of Christ' is rather a characterization of its meritorious author than the relation of grace itself, which alone brings man face to face with God. Christ's role as mediator is not incorporated into man's existential relation to God and experience of grace, and remains a point in distant history. Despite this critical reservation, we can appreciate Anselm's soteriology with greater justice. It has more to say to the modern theory of redemption than is often supposed.

3   The Anabaptists[4]

For many years it was customary to concentrate on the reforming policies of Luther, Calvin, and Zwingli. Church history and the history of theology paid scant attention either to the forerunners of the Reformation or to its fringe phenomena. A more critical approach to Luther's version of Christianity and to the consequences of his theory of justification emerged only when theology tried to achieve (in part) the perspective of the Marxist critique of religion and inquired more searchingly into the social relevance of faith and theology. Luther's rejection of justification by works was not, of course, intended to lead to an undervaluation of human activity and a neglect of ethics, but his theory of justification, so strongly stamped with his own experiences, effectively limited the ethical perspective to the individual person and the area of individual moral behaviour, in which the fruits of the new life of faith were supposed to be seen. A critical reflection on its social and political relevance helped, admittedly, to release the Church from government by the hierarchy and clergy (one of the errors attributed to the Catholic Church). But this political order was then replaced by the juridical order of the local prince and his government, justified by Christian obedience to lawful authority. Recent discussion of the so-called theory of the two kingdoms has absolved Luther himself from various misinterpretations and misuses of the theory. Releasing the political arena from ecclesiastical control and giving independence to political reason spared society the legal and violent satisfaction of the eschatological demands of the Evangelicals. But it must not be misconstrued as a willingness to exclude political life from the responsibility of conscience and from the eschatological and present lordship of Christ. Despite this, the theory of the two kingdoms has remained susceptible to a static juxtaposition of the two realms in which there is no contact, much less unity. As the Lutheran Reformation became increasingly tied to the rule of princes and the structures of bourgeois municipal organization, the conservative tendency of the Lutheran ethos in relation to society became stronger.

The Church's extension of Christian ethics to the social arena, and the eschatological relativization and greater possibility of change in existing social structures, has directed the attention of theologians not only to this conservative ethos, but even more to fringe movements of the Reformation period. Some surprising ideas and certain adumbrations of later opinions have been discovered. Lochman, for example, has emphasized the fact that the Reformation in Bohemia, under Hus, was from the start a movement of the lower classes. In their brotherhoods and in their relations with the local authorities these classes developed a sense of independence and even of aggression. As a result of coupling the Bohemian too readily with the wider Lutheran Reformation, historians long lost sight of this difference, although never perhaps totally.

The wider effect of Luther's Reformation had even more damaging consequences for Thomas Müntzer's Baptist movement. Unlike Luther, Müntzer contrasted the words of Scripture with a man's own spiritual experience, in which Christian proclamation reaches its true goal. Further, he laid greater stress on the justified Christian's new way of life, of which, in his view, Luther took too little account. Above all, he brought the eschatological horizon of God's Kingdom much more forcefully into the present, subordinating to it not only the behaviour of the individual but also social and political institutions and the princes their supporters. With prophetic strength he applied Daniel's vision of the world's kingdoms to contemporary history. His penitential sermons not only dealt with the private world of faith, but also subordinated the political use of power to the claims of the gospel and made its legitimacy dependent on the gospel: 'Where you do not do this, you shall be put to the sword'.[5] It is understandable that such preaching found a ready audience among the poor and exploited peasants and frightened the princes. Other forces, of course, contributed to the Baptist and later peasant revolts, but Müntzer gave them a spirituality of their own. Luther's opinion was that this extension of the Christian's freedom was no more than fanaticism and disorder, and he denounced it accordingly.

Outside Christian theology, this current of the Reformation has been taken up especially by E. Bloch[6] and, with other phenomena of ecclesiastical history, raised to the level of nothing less than a 'tradition of subversion'. According to Bloch, Müntzer failed to draw the ultimate consequences of his principles, otherwise he would have been led to question radically his own religious presuppositions. The critical relativization of earthly authority would have been continued in a critique of God's authority, whereas in fact Müntzer regarded the latter as the legitimation of the former. Bloch even suggests that Müntzer laid claim to a religious motivation on merely tactical gounds. This view, however, is generally rejected as an unhistorical interpretation of Müntzer's statements. His ethical summons can be understood only as the product of his own spiritual experience and religious fervour. The defeat of the Anabaptist movement left Lutheranism lacking for many years the critical alternative to its own conservative and restorative attitude, and in fact reinforced that attitude.

4 Religious Socialism[7]

The industrialization and consequent misery of the proletariat contributed to the formation of a socialist movement. Although the movement found in the churches isolated and vociferous supporters who tried to discover a solution to the social question, the socialist movement gathered its main momentum outside those churches. Further, because the bourgeoisie justified and defended its right of ownership with religious concepts of order, and fought for the retention of the existing order as an ideological mission, socialism became an opponent of the Church and of Christianity. It was now easy for the bourgeoisie to defame socialism for its 'unchristianity', even in its legitimate social postulates, and consequently to idealize itself as a constituent of the Christian order. It is difficult

43

to decide how far ideological education was cause or effect of the social opposition.

It is certain that a movement such as Religious Socialism can be attributed only to the conservatism of the great churches. If criticism and the remedy of social grievances had found a more ready response in the Church in Germany and Switzerland, as they did for example in England, the attempt to deal with the misfortunes of the proletariat and the question of work would have taken a different course. In Germany and Switzerland there were only a few campaigners such as Kutter and Ragaz, who proposed social work that went beyond the removal of individual evils and tackled the improvement of legal and social structures. The members and leaders of the churches saw the socialists en bloc as hostile to the faith and, from the bourgeois-nationalist point of view, as people without a fatherland. The beginnings were marked by the programme set out by the younger Ch. Blumhardt, who acknowledged Jesus not only as Lord in the soul of the individual but also as a victor over the demonic forces threatening the state and society, who inaugurates God's Kingdom not at some point beyond this world but in the world of here and now. He did not equate the socialist movement with the Kingdom of God, but he thought that it pursued God's work in as much as it stood for peace, justice, and harmony. The physical nature of salvation, of which the Bible speaks, was in his view better preserved by socialism than by the view that limited salvation to some spiritual or private area of life.

In Switzerland, where the reformed type of Protestantism was more open to ethical conduct in politics, Kutter and Ragaz in particular tried to gain understanding and opportunity for the socialist movement by reminding Christians of its evangelical source and by reproaching the churches for their one-sided and ultimately ineffective proclamation of justification. The reader is referred here, by way of example, to Kutter's book *Sie müssen. Ein offenes Wort an die christliche Gesellschaft* (1903). God is present not only where he is revered in religion and cult; he is wherever his will is done in the struggle for justice. Religious Socialism did not intend to reduce the gospel to a system of ethics by trying to make it once again socially relevant.

44

Kutter and Ragaz did not identify socialism and the Kingdom of God, but regarded the former as a movement preparatory for the latter.

Instead of the hitherto central doctrine of justification, which could lead to a quietistic attitude towards God's exclusive work and to a suspicion of ethical conduct, they placed the Sermon on the Mount and active discipleship at the centre of their theology and publicity: 'The Sermon on the Mount will again stand out. Stronger and more impetuous than ever. It is obscured by so-called justification by faith ... then the cause of Christ goes rapidly into decline'.[8] They rescued the Sermon on the Mount from the weakening pictures of it to which it had been subjected at the hands of an inner, spiritual, or élitist and monastic interpretation. Eschatological realism explained God's Kindom as changing theocracy. While the more quietist Kutter retired in shock at the First World War, the more active Ragaz continued his rhetorical and populist educational work. He reproached dialectical theology, which shared with Religious Socialism an interest in eschatology, for fleeing the world and withdrawing into theology. Meanwhile Religious Socialism had found adherents and representatives in Germany: G. Wünsch, for example, who accused Lutheranism of neglecting the social implications of Christianity, and P. Tillich, who desired to see the Unconditioned realized not only in the area of 'religion'.

The perversion of the socialist utopia by the Russian revolution and its perpetuation under Soviet dictatorship and by the ever more determined effort of the churches to isolate and hinder Religious Socialism allowed the latter less and less space in which to function. It is only fair, however, that the memory of these precursors should be preserved in today's debates on political theology, on the social relevance of the gospel, and on its eschatological message. They must not be judged merely for their theological bias and oversimplification, much less for their failure in Church and society. Their great service was to proclaim to a bourgeois ecclesiastical mentality the social summons of the gospel. Their misfortune was to experience how loath the Church was to be reminded of the radical nature of her origins.

5

Redemption in the context of man's search for meaning[1]

The present chapter deals with some new interpretations of Christian belief concerning salvation, which share a markedly anthropocentric bias but locate and articulate the question of meaning in very different ways. The present emphasis of theological reflection on subjectivity, existence, and personal experience does not necessarily lead to the neglect or reduction of God's 'objective' reality and historical salvific activity. Similarly, tradition should not be accused, merely because of its stronger emphasis on the personal source of salvation, of having employed objectifying patterns of thought and speech. The soteriological correlation admits of different ideologically conditioned centres of gravity.

Soteriology, too, more than any other department of theology, has always been aware of this anthropological correlation and preserved it throughout the several periods and systems of theology. It is in soteriology if anywhere that the believer, with his experience of sin and expectation of salvation, must be included in the picture. There, God and his acts cannot be spoken of so 'objectively' that man and his history are excluded from consideration. Thus the modern emphasis on the subject and his relationship to God (or to Christ and the Christ-event) cannot be regarded as something entirely new. It would be more accurate to see in the original offer to man of salvation and revelation one of the factors that have inevitably contributed to modern anthropocentrism. Other factors include the critical analysis of the conditions of human knowledge and their influence of man's relation to the world and reality, and an awareness of the historical relativity of human experience and interpretation of the world. This experience cannot be located at the same level as the effects and causes of natural laws ranging man as one earthly object amongst others. No, man's conscious and free attitude to reality is essential to reality's shape and expression. The reason why anthropocentrism in theology has turned out so variously is that the correlative reality of God was not clear in a secularized world and therefore could be investigated only after the corresponding relation of man.

There is another element, which has also hastened secularization. Man is now offered other possibilities for the significant fulfilment of his humanity. On the horizon formerly constituted by the all-pervading light of God's reality there are now other landmarks making similar claims and offers. The question of man's origin and destiny, of the ground of his existence, can now also be answered from non-religious viewpoints. Christian belief in salvation has to defend itself in the face of these many possible meanings in human life. It must submit to the same linguistic and language-game rules which apply to them. In the context of these various directions of human questioning, the problem is to ensure that the Christian message of salvation does not deliberately ignore or fail to notice man's search for meaning, but offers it an intelligible answer.

1 *Mediations of soteriological immediacy*
Belief concerning salvation needs to be reinterpreted because the usual answers presume and appeal to an unquestioned immediacy in man's relation to God. This conflicts with the tendency of modern man to determine his position using other co-ordinates and other landmarks. God as the term of man's basic relationships yields to other correlative aims and origins which are internal to the world and history. Man now defines himself not so much in his relation to God as in his relation to other people, to his own existence, to the future, and so on. Most concepts and confessions of this belief arose and were formulated before the immediacy of man's relation to God was ever questioned. The language reflects this. Man is guilty before God; God forgives sins; because of his slavery to sin, man is not free to do God's will; he is condemned for transgressing God's law, he loses hope but is granted eternal life by God, divine sonship in grace in Jesus Christ, and the brotherly community of belief in the Church. From the New Testament

47

onward, those are the ideas that have dominated Christian tradition. They are supposed to explain the conflicts and contradictions in the world and the particular ways in which the Church offers her service of reconciliation and the gift of salvation. The problem is that in daily living and in man's social relationships they are now hardly part of his experience: his conflicts and his expectation of salvation are located elsewhere. However, it does not follow that the main content of Christian belief concerning salvation is proved worthless; it is now applied to human existentials within the world and between people, losing its 'religious' tenor. Guilt and forgiveness are now regarded as separating and reconciling not God and man but man and man. The law governing human conscience is no longer thought of as the divine command but as that dictated by the demands of society, without the prior satisfaction of which man cannot achieve integrity. He has to do 'good works' (= things positively achieved) in order to be justified before this court. Unfreedom and slavery are no longer thought to be due directly to demonic powers or God's wrath; they lie much closer to man's heart, in his own anxieties and constraints, in the unredeemed conflicts and repressions of his own soul. Many of the traditional designations are to all appearances verbally retained and command the same respect as before, but they are really the vocabulary of psychology and the social sciences. We may justly speak of a 'migration' of experiences of sin and of expectations of salvation, apparent also in the 'migration' to secularized forms and bearers of salvation. Is there, at the root of this shift in belief concerning salvation, also a real though hidden new kind of experience of sin and salvific expectation, assigning a new field to interpretation of the message of salvation? Can the Christian proclamation of salvation introduce its traditional revelation of sin and its promise of eternal healing into these new mediated experiences without adapting to an ephemeral vogue and yet without talking about something totally different and alien?

2   *The anthropological substratum of the experience of sin and salvation*[3]

Soteriology is pursued and articulated from the standpoint of

48

the subject both in theological tradition and in the modern quest for meaning. But given the shift in the correlative realities, the question arises whether agreement in taking the subject as a pivotal point of discussion allows us to speak of the same experience even in the same subject, or whether in the two cases the same subject is addressed and intended in different ways and affected at different levels of experience. If analogous situations in other areas of theology are anything to go by, we can suspect *a priori* that opinions lie between two extremes. In fundamental theology, for example, man as the subject of belief is either totally divorced from man as the subject of other religious experiences or identified without qualification. In the first case, theology will claim to address man in a unique way as the subject of sin and salvation, without anywhere needing to encounter other anthropological forms of this experience. It will not, naturally, conflict with any formulations of the search for meaning that lie outside explicit Christian belief. The experience of guilt and forgiveness has nothing in common with the findings and interpretations of, say, psychology. Nor can an exclusively theological soteriology be troubled by the questions and criticisms of other human sciences. However, the present situation shows that this isolation of theology, in which contact and conflict alike are absent, has vanished, since dialectical theology proved, on the whole, a dangerous weakening of the relation of faith and reality. Belief in the uniqueness and exclusiveness of faith and its way of looking at things, however sincerely held, and, at the personal level, the mystification of the Christian's experiences of sin and salvation as exclusively Spirit-wrought experiences must not be allowed to deceive us. In the second case, theology is faced with the grave question whether its own perspective and language are really any different from what other human sciences and methods of healing say and do in their own ways more pertinently and competently, without any confusing superstructure of metaphysics. Several recent soteriological interpretations, trying to get away from the unreal theological jargon of sin and salvation and to speak to man from within his spiritual and social experience, move between these two alternatives. They find themselves increasingly faced with a major difficulty. How can they maintain the inalienable uniqueness and originality of Christian belief in salvation and continue to draw on the data and methods of the human sciences? We have already mentioned a 'migration' of specifically Christian concepts into areas of general human experience; for example, when people talk of guilt and reconciliation, slavery and redemption, in areas of individual and social concern. We can also notice a reverse movement in which categories from psychology and sociology are reinterpreted and applied in theological soteriology: identity, integration, acceptance of one's shadow, and so on. The concern here is to give otherwise empty theological descriptions of the subject a solid substratum of meaning, and conversely to give psychological diagnoses the aura of credal statements. Theologians are also concerned to allow the methods of psychology and sociology to partake of the quality of the real grace-filled salvific event. The exclusion from psychology of problems posed by transcendence and immanence creates particular difficulties: how do the mental, symbolic objectifications of religious or ethical experience relate to the personal correlates from which faith sees salvation originating? To put this question the other way round, what significance have the correlates God and Jesus Christ in the sphere of pre-given mental realities, both individual and collective? Finally, how can the processes of grace-given forgiveness and new obedience in faith be combined with the processes and struggles of man's maturity on his way to spiritual recovery? The partial identity of terminology does not yet give any guarantee that the basic differences between psychology and psychotherapy on the one hand and theology and pastoral care on the other are even known, much less resolved.

3   *Human experience of self as the (anonymous) Christian experience of grace*[4]

Criticism of traditional soteriology has included soteriology's independence of dogmatic Christology, which in its turn was devoid of soteriological relevance. The hypostatic union, the inner reality of Christ, seemed to be no more than an objective statement of fact, at best a preliminary to the proper work of salvation. It confronted the believer as a unique, exceptional event to which man had no access in his understanding and much less, of course, in his experience. The renewal of Christ-ology has tried to break down this isolation. Christ's inner being must be interpreted as a reality already salvific in itself, and a way offered to man, in his own earthbound experience of spirit and freedom, of gaining some understanding of it. Karl Rahner has suggested an analogy between man's transcenden-tal experience of self and the unity of Christ. He not only describes the latter at the ontic level, but also raises it to the existential height of human awareness and freedom. He is able not only to point to a deeper continuity between the linguisti-cally disparate systems of Christology in the New Testament and a primitive dogma, but also to introduce the unique hypostatic union into man's horizon of understanding. The common line of approach is man's openness to God and transcendence of the world. Jesus Christ, and man generally, look to God as to the mystery of all reality. The mystery constantly confronts man with the question whether God as the hidden ground of all reality always remains hidden or some-times communicates himself to man in grace. Man cannot answer this question of himself, but in Christ God's uncondi-tioned freedom has been revealed as a freedom that communicates itself. Christ's ontic unity, therefore, consists of God's total self-communication to Jesus in grace and man's God-given openness to God in self-transcendence. From this surpassing fulness, intelligible from within his own experience of self, man can turn back to himself with a better and redeemed understanding. In Christ he has seen the original ground of his own existence and met it in faith. He must also hope to meet in his own transcen-dence of self the God who gives himself unreservedly. His infinite, and therefore world-transcending, desire cannot re-main for ever unappeased.

This mutual openness of Jesus's experience of self and of God has not only added a new dimension to man's experience of transcendence, which in earlier theology had been called 'natural', but has also brought Jesus's experience of God into closer union with the ebb and flow of the human experience of God. If the unity of Jesus with God is understood in purely ontic terms, the effort to preserve the human drama of Jesus's life loses all credibility. If, on the other hand, that same unity is viewed dynamically as a conscious and free relationship to God which can also reach and subsume the definitive nature of Christ's divine sonship, then there is no obligation to postulate a constant, ultimately unhistorical, beatific vision on Christ's part. Rather, the opposition between death and resurrection can now be extended to God's hiddenness and revelation. Man must now know that his experience of God is transferred from anxiety to trust and wrapped in trust.

Although there are some inconsistencies of christological structure in such an up-dating of ontic Christology into a Christology of consciousness and freedom, it must be complimented for achieving its two goals. The constitution of Christ in the incarnation and hypostatic union is articulated in a way that reveals its soteriological content without any further additions. No complicated transformation is needed to create a possibility of understanding between man's experience of self and the mystery of God's incarnation in Christ. Belief in the mystery is no easier, but it has gained in clarity and salvific meaning.

4 *Christology as the implicit horizon of interhuman encounter*[5]

One of the features of the modern search for meaning is that it is no longer oriented directly to man's relationship with God, but starts from the acceptance or rejection of one's own person by those about one. Man's orientation to his social environment, as portrayed in the psychology of development, is no longer primarily anthropological and existential. Man becomes aware of himself in leaving himself and encountering others. That encounter determines the success or failure of his self-discovery, self-acceptance, and personal history. Conversely, the world and history, and also the claim of absolute values and realities, centre on man. Even though it is not suggested that this mediation is so exclusive as to make a personal relationship and dialogue between man and God impossible, even though, therefore, man's relationships are not wholly accounted for by others, others cannot be passed by. Any reinterpretation of soteriology must take this self-understanding into account and not direct man to an immediate relationship with God which he finds it almost impossible to achieve. It will rather look to traditional belief concerning salvation for ideas and forerunners of a similarly dimensioned quest for salvation, even though complete correspondence to the present spiritual situation is not to be expected. Rather, this hermeneutical gap can give rise to a critical questioning of man's present predominant experience of self and open it to a relationship with God.

Now the unity of love of God with love of neighbour in the preaching of Jesus (Mark 12.31; Matt. 19.19; Rom. 13.9) had not escaped the notice of New Testament exegetes and moral theologians. Nor had the counsel that made Christ's loving self-effacement the rule and motive force of charity (1 Cor. 8.11; 1 John 3.16; etc.). But love of one's neighbour could as it were support itself on love of God, whereas today it is more likely to be found on its own. Furthermore, there was very little reflection on the anthropological connection of the two relationships; they were simply considered to be held together by the one commandment. Now, however, their intimate nexus and its christological basis are very much in view. In Jesus's own attitudes, in his preaching, parables, and ministry, the advent of the Kingdom of God, the approach of God's love and his urgent appeal, was not simply an event that took place in vertical immediacy between God and man. It arose in the encounter with Jesus, in the relationship of the disciples with each other, in the early community, and ultimately in every human encounter. The inner nature of love is experienced, offered, and made possible in my contacts with others. The questioning and neediness of my fellow men confronts me with God's unconditional claims. Anyone who wished to wait for both on a direct encounter with God would long since have closed his mind to the presence of God in his own fellows. In opposing any restriction of faith and obedience to explicit cultic piety or fulfilment of the law, Jesus identified true service of God with one's duties to one's fellow men, the relief of suffering, and service to the least of one's brothers. One is tempted to reproach Jesus himself—as indeed the new soteriology itself has been unjustifiably reproached—with having shifted the centre of gravity, 'horizontalizing' the love of God.

There are, of course, many nuances among these new

soteriological theories, ranging from a balanced integration of love of God and love of one's neighbour to an undialectical identification in which 'God' seems to be no more than a cipher for the claims made on one's conscience by one's neighbour. We must observe where the path of love of neighbour as the road to God is kept open to someone who is not yet a believer as an authentic road on which, sooner or later, he will search for the absolute ground and significance of his neighbour, and where, by identifying the two virtues, the question of God as the mystery present in every encounter is rendered superfluous. A complete independence would neglect the relationship with God, which Jesus regarded as essential, and the love and demands inherent in God's Kingdom. This objection must be made to the attempt to make independent the I-must and I-should. H. Braun, for example, thus represents Jesus's grace-filled address and the claims he makes through the neighbour, and sees them completely restored to intelligibility in a post-theistic age.[6] But because for Jesus the reality of the Father is the true ground and empowering source of his own mission and preaching, if that reality is eliminated his ministry loses not simply a time-conditioned background but its very roots. Detached from this living relation to God, Jesus's beatitudes and promises stand as mere pious wishes, and, excluded from the liberating and consoling gospel, his commandments become crippling, imperious laws. It would be an oversimplification of the unity of the commandment to love God and one's neighbour to deny that the latter continually arises from the former and transcends itself to reach the former. The absoluteness of love is bearable both for the neighbour who encounters me and for myself only because of love of God. Without this horizon, even though more often implicit than explicit, it would be an intolerable burden.

5 *The future as goal of the quest for meaning*[7]

The modern search for the significance of human life differs from the earlier search not only in its more reserved, transcendental alignment, but also in its historical direction. Of course the location of one's own life and activity in time has always been one of the essential co-ordinates of the interpretation of meaning and orientation: where do we come from, where are we going? The significance of the here-and-now, the succession of days and years, depended on the answer to those questions. The accelerated development of man's technical and rational potentialities, the violence of political evolution that swamps the individual, and the daily relativization of those certainties that still exist have led to a dominance of the future in man's relation to time. The question 'where to?' has become much more important than the question 'where from?'. Times of optimistic preoccupation with the future, however, and the possibilities it offers alternate rapidly with times of pessimistic fear of a future that eludes us or is already decided for us by anonymous forces. The secularized experience of history has changed the transcendent future into goals that remain within the world and history. Again, the search for salvation cannot remain impervious to its influence.

It is no longer sufficient to counter this postion with the eschatological hope revealed in Jesus's proclamation of the Kingdom and in his own resurrection. If secularization has limited its horizon to a future confined to history and the world, it will simply scale down the all-encompassing future to secular proportions. The position, however, has helped to find in Jesus's preaching and in the Early Church's experience of the risen and glorified Lord not only similar questions but also similar answers. The future of God's Kingdom or the resurrection of Jesus not only has an objective component but is also brought to bear on man's existence and subjectivity, where it is less a question of the ultimate extent of the disclosed future than of including the future in man's present. The eschatological future leads man out of the present hopeless situation, gives him a possibility of new life, and frees him from the oppressive burden of his sinful and mortal past. Only this existential interpretation enables the promise of God's Kingdom and of resurrection to affect man and lead him out of his enclosed history, as in the cures of the sick, the forgiveness of sinners, the beatitudes of the Sermon on the Mount, the communication of life on the part of the Johannine Jesus. When attention is paid not to the overall *content* of the future embodied in these statements or its symbolic description ('Kingdom of God', 'eternal life') but to the general future *direction* indicated, we are nearer to bringing together the question of meaning (in the form of the question of the future) on the one hand and Jesus's promise of hope on the other.

The question of meaning, which is theologically unanswerable in its secularized form without further qualification, has obliged us to carry out an existential hermeneutic of the biblical promise, and has disclosed a meaning previously unsought and therefore not found. If we unite this historical mediation with the previously mentioned mediation of interhuman encounter, the individual has a greater duty—and ability—to offer his fellow men the service of revealing this newly opened future, a service that will also open up the future for himself.

6

The political dimension of salvation[1]

Development of the political aspects of salvation has posed a new problem for the reinterpretation of soteriology. Those aspects had, of course, been present all along. Man's sin and salvation had always had political repercussions; the new questions were first raised not by theology but by the critical analysis of social structures and forces undertaken by political philosophy and social theory. But sooner or later theology had to realize that in its understanding of salvation it was dealing with man as he is, in his multiple social relationships and structures, that the Church's preaching and pastoral praxis could therefore not ignore this dimension of man without a damaging loss of relevance and effectiveness. The whole question arises from an area of reflection hitherto unknown to Christian tradition; hence it cannot be answered from tradition without a recognition of the hermeneutical gap. Our purpose now is to trace the social problems in this tradition, even where they were not noticed and articulated as such. Our hope is cautiously to draw from this implication explicit statements and contributions to this modern problem. We must be aware of the gap that separates not only the areas of implicit and explicit social reflection but also, and to a much greater degree, the situation of Christianity in political circumstances other than those of the secularized (if not always de-ideologized) state. To what extent can we today expect clarification of a concrete political problem —the question of military service, for example—from Jesus's attitudes in an occupied country, without wresting individual biblical statements from their historical and social context and transplanting them into a totally alien culture? On the other hand, political theology, understood as a reflection and realization of Christian belief in the context of modern society, could not and cannot ignore this considerable hermeneutical difference and thus run the risk of misinterpretation and misjudgement because of an initial and basic unwillingness to face the problem.

1   *The critique of apolitical tradition as a*
    'tendency to privatize'[2]

Political theology started primarily as a critique of types of
theology in which politics was neglected or entirely ignored. Its
development was furthered by certain pressing social decisions.
These decisions were a challenge to Christians and the churches,
and theologians wished to avoid the mistakes of the past. Political theology's definition was at first, then, a statement of what
it did not intend to be.

Traditional theology, especially its soteriology, lay open to
the charge that the service it claimed to offer man was in fact
given to people of reduced and abstract proportions because
their social determinations were excluded. This charge of being
apolitical in the theory and praxis of salvation can be levelled at
all concepts which, in the course of history, have impaired the
original wholeness of salvation as based in the Old Testament
expectation of salvation and in the dawning of eschatological
salvation in Jesus. This judgement also includes concepts which
have failed to take account of other human dimensions, those,
for example, which talk exclusively in terms of 'salvation of the
soul' or display a privatistic concern for the salvation of the
individual. It also embraces those interpretations of salvation
which summon the individual to decision from the anonymity of
the masses. An example would be the existentialist interpretation, in which 'the many' are merely the obscure and dispensable background for the existence of the individual, who
alone truly makes decisions. A similar criticism must be made of
a well-intentioned social ethic which considers the person as self-
transcending in his communication with the 'thou' of his fellow
man but limits his social intercourse to primary social forms
such as the family and other less structured communities. The
theologian does not come to grips with the political dimension
until he turns his attention directly to society, with its complex
institutional structures, authorities, and forms of organization.
Society thus considered is more than the sum of the simple
forms of community or the numberless interhuman relationships of which it consists. This can also be seen negatively in the
fact that this dimension is reached in both critique and praxis,

not by the sum of individual ethical appeals or efforts by social ethics to relate to society, but only by tackling the process of legislation and the creation or removal of institutional authority. There are factors of sin not affected by the personal conversion of the individual. There is service to man's salvation when social, cultural, or ecclesial political relationships are healed even without short-term acts of charity in the tradition of the Good Samaritan. Even though this type of service does not enjoy the glamour and respectful acknowledgement of public acclaim, it is no less a field of ethical decision and responsibility. Here the strongly personal nature of traditional soteriology, and also, paradoxically, of theological ethics, was a hindrance because it could not discern in more abstract political work the human face of this or that individual. And yet the individual is no less affected, for better or worse, by changes in these structures.

2   The theological reception of the political dimension[3]

Various historical experiences might partly explain why theology had withdrawn from this area and consequently lost sight of the political dimension. In the Middle Ages, when Church and state were so closely allied, the Church had less need to concern herself with political interests, because these were taken care of by the state, of which she was herself an integral part. The Church adopted a critical attitude only when she saw her own independence and freedom of action threatened. A similar 'harmony' between crown and altar encouraged the reformed churches to neglect the political arena. The polemical emancipation of the state from ecclesiastical domination further excluded the Church from politics and persuaded her that her proper activity was pastoral care of the individual. Finally, theology remained opposed to politics so as not to be numbered in the questionable ranks of a clericalistic 'political Catholicism'; she had to draw her justification from elsewhere.

When theology as a whole had begun to think more in terms of mankind and had recognized that anthropocentrism was a latent or manifest intention of biblical revelation and the history of salvation, the inclusion of politics was not far away. To exclude it would have been to limit salvation and God's Kingdom.

How could a 'salvation' which, in order to save man, had first to pluck him from his social context deserve the name? The need to safeguard the integrity of man and his world by including the political dimension was imposed no less imperiously from another quarter. At almost the same time as political theology, eschatology was becoming a major factor in theological thought. The eschatological horizon was not limited to an other-worldly frontier, but cast a critical and promise-laden light over the entire field of human reality, particularly where conditions seemed least to warrant it. Enslaving social conditions must not be excepted. Between these two poles—theological anthropology and eschatology—Christology and ecclesiology gained a new insight: the assumption and redemption of man in Chalcedonian homoousia now included *solidarity* with man, not as an abstract individual or collective 'nature' but as a historical and social being. The Church's witness and service could not overlook this concrete social reality that was to be redeemed no less surely than the individual.

The occasional criticism that political theology was introducing into soteriology categories and a terminology that were foreign to it is thus rebutted. The original impulse may have been from earlier theories and movements critical of, and intent on changing, society; but this impulse from outside was soon accepted and fortified by a movement from within the very heart of the faith.

Political theology has shown, above all, that ultimately there is no neutral, apolitical alternative. Where theology and Church exclude the political dimension of man, they contribute, knowingly or unknowingly, to the conservation of existing political relationships.

3   The mutual relationship of theory and praxis[4]

The openness and willingness of political theology to deal with a type of science that has behind it a tradition and evolution completely different from the sciences on which theology previously drew have had another important consequence. Hitherto, in theology, the pattern has been from theory to practical realization. Each discipline followed a set procedure, starting with the biblical data and the history of dogma and

Church life, continuing with a systematic reflection on those data and concluding by handing on the theoretical results to practical or pastoral theology. Whenever there were contrary movements—for example, from liturgical practice to theological reflection in the theology of the sacraments—this excursion into the realm of praxis was cut short and theology diverted back to the mainstream of theory-to-practice.

Meanwhile, the social theory of Marxism had disclosed the connection between social relationships on the one hand, consciousness and thought on the other. It had criticized the conception of ideology as the consequence and expression of social relationships or interests. Theory was conditioned by praxis more thoroughly than it knew. As far as this critique of ideology is concerned, there was a positive side. It was possible that a new practice could lead to the invention of a new theory, that praxis opened up possibilities of thought to which pure theory would have been blind. And the same praxis could show an established theory to be false.

Even though we cannot here detail the various stages in this contrary process, we must remark on this revolution in theological method which has become a general characteristic of political theology. Political theology does not first develop theoretical models, which it compares with present praxis, and then criticize or alter that praxis accordingly. It starts from experience, from actual activities, such as the Latin-American liberation movement, and then proceeds to criticize and correct the theory.[5] This methodological change has also proved fruitful in the rest of theology, and not only on the postulate of a theological study related to praxis!

4   *Development of an implicit political theology*[6]

The term 'political theology' and the categories it employs are new, but the resulting research has inaugurated a vision of the biblical sources and theological tradition which has brought to light some surprising aspects.

The Old Covenant and its ordinances are correctly viewed only when interpreted as the vital ordering of Israel and that people's economic and social problems. Exegetes had tended to concentrate on this life as a whole, while the rest of theology had scrutinized the Old Testament for its specifically theological statements. The critique undertaken by the prophets as well as the promise of a new order were not restricted to the private or interhuman, but also concerned themselves with social and legal relationships. And even this political level remained subordinate to the theological relationship or promise of the covenant. The theological component of the covenant and of the law was expressed in the commandments. Conversely, the commandments were ordered to the people's basic relation to God.

The picture of Jesus takes on new features. There is no question of again representing Jesus as a political revolutionary; but the figure of an apolitical Jesus, busied only with interiority and the individual person, is equally false. Even though he did not intend to overthrow political or social relationships, his eschatological preaching and its practice had an explosive power which produced political effects and conflicts. The defensive tactics of official Judaism and the Roman Empire cannot be described as results of mere misunderstanding. The observer who was profoundly shocked by the preaching and praxis of Jesus in relation to the Jewish law, to the system of social classes, to the powerful of this world, was not deceived. The resistance to Jesus, which did not begin with individuals loath to believe in him, but enlisted the co-operation of men who were pillars of society and guarantors of the law, permits us to conclude that Jesus issued a call to justice and conversion which transcended the individual and his activity.

With his sabbath healings and meals with all classes of society, Jesus did not merely perform a few signs; he shook the fabric of Jewish society itself. This was included in the charge brought by his accusers. The reaction to him, not only an individual but a strongly political reaction, shows that, even though his conduct was designed to inaugurate something more than a new political movement, it had that effect also. Jesus's death on the cross was not merely a victory of individual unbelief and disobedience; it was the maintenance and continuation of the social *status quo*, which parried with death Jesus's threat to its own life. The resurrection of Jesus denied authority not only to the individual doer but also to the law, to the whole structure of society which

62

motivated him. Paul rightly dramatized Calvary as the legal pronouncement invalidating the law itself (Rom. 10.4; 1 Cor. 15.56; Gal. 3.13).

The cosmic setting of the cross is even clearer in the captivity epistles. The cross reconciles not only man and God but also Greek and Jew (Eph. 2.11–21). Those to whom salvation is offered and who benefit therefrom are not individuals only but ethnic groups who had up till then been excluded from Israel. The one body of the crucified and risen Christ now unites the separated and brings strangers together. Sin and salvation extend to social structures. Where the captivity epistles personify and mythologize by subordinating to Christ's rule the 'powers and dominations' which spread and maintain deception and self-seeking in the world (Col. 2.14–16), political theology can now demythologize and talk of social structures broken by Christ's liberating kingship. God's eschatological kingship denies the intra-worldly powers the omnipotence they claim; but it also places the efforts to achieve a just society and a redeemed humanity under an 'eschatological proviso'. On the whole, political theology has been more successful in achieving its negative, critical aims than in providing individual Christians and the Church generally with positive directives for social action. It has tended to camouflage with amateur political activity the danger of intervening in highly complex matters without the necessary competence, on the sole plea of theological motivation. Sooner or later it must leave the area of general principles and develop imperatives.

5 *Political theology as the hermeneutic of redemption*[7]

Political theology occupies an uneasy position between the biblical and traditional theologoumena of soteriology on the one hand and the various secularized but not unideological social theories on the other. It must not only mediate between two different languages but effectively introduce a pre-reflexive, unarticulated, politically irrelevant soteriology into the debate with developed and considered social theories. The combination and employment of two languages not only poses a serious hermeneutical problem; it can also involve a considerable risk. Will theology be harnessed to an already established political postulate which can be just as well motivated without theology? Conversely, will political differences of opinion be obscured or precipitately resolved by resorting to theological categories? Or does political theology promote a fruitful dialogue between the ways in which faith and a secularized, even atheistic, humanism look at man? The social context determines the main questions asked and will take from theology the nearest ethical props. To be properly understood, however, such theological postulates need a whole context. Will they still be correctly made when isolated from that context, detached from God's gracious, free deeds in Jesus Christ and regarded only as demands, not as gestures which also enable those demands to be fulfilled? In general it is easier for political hermeneutic to draw on the critique and demands of the gospel when it does not go too deeply into the basis for those demands: God's gracious and elevating activity. However, the ethical consequences of Easter are not the same detached from the Easter-event.

As an example of a finely differentiated and balanced interpretation, we may mention Kessler's attempt[8] to combine the motivation and aims of Christian salvific activity with those of atheistic liberation theory. First of all, the biblical statement of God's salvific initiative and fulfilment is almost meaningless to a liberation theory in which freedom is achieved by man and with human aims: man appears to take God's place quite adequately. In a directly theological soteriology there seems to be no room for man's own responsibility and aims; in an exclusively anthropocentric soteriology there is no room for a divine initiative and completion. This incompatibility can change and lead to the possibility of mutual understanding if both sides abandon their exclusive claims. For example, it is an oversimplification for Christian soteriology to present God's initiative, which is intended to save man and call on his co-operation, exclusively as God's work. The fact that the gracious indicative of God's liberation and the imperative of change in man's newly bestowed freedom go together does not, of course, deny their distinction, but it does forbid any simplification in favour of God or man. Liberation theory too, however, has its own difficulties, at least in the minds of some of its more self-critical proponents. They are unable to say whence and why liberation should be inaugurated, in what particulars the existing order is inadequate, and what motive power is to lie behind the attempt to transcend it. They cannot offer as their aim simply the finite sum of all human desires. They find themselves led to postulate the human desire for the Wholly Other beyond all attainable and attained objectives. Although Kessler does not immediately fill this void by introducing the Christian notion of God, he discerns at least a possibility of mutual understanding. Liberation theory and Christian belief concerning salvation point in the same direction. As long as this dialogue remains open, we cannot justly speak, as unfortunately some critics do, of an estrangement between Christian salvation-belief and political movements.

6   Political ecclesiology[9]

Discussion of the political cannot be restricted to the sphere of secular activity; the Church herself must be critically analysed as a social organism, particularly as to whether, and if so to what extent, structures of unfreedom, discrimination, and falsehood persist notwithstanding the best intentions of her individual members, even her officials, and despite repeated calls to inner conversion. The foundation of the Church by Christ and her animation by the Spirit offer no adequate information about her as a social entity which, despite its transcendent origin within history, is constructed of human language with the help of human forms of organization. The distinction between the Spirit-filled Church and her social shape is not intended to revive that between a visible and an invisible Church. But it enables us to see that the Church's various juridical structures, which have changed throughout history, are relative. They embody, perhaps, a *ius divinum*, but they cannot be credited with divine immutability.

Apart from the nature of the Church as a society, political ecclesiology would consider the mutual relations between the Church and the national, economic, cultural, and social forms of life around her. The relationship is frequently far from clearcut; it is often more of an osmosis than a juxtaposition of isolated bodies. To what extent are ecclesiastical structures reflections of historical organizations of the state, say in feudal times, with a

65

mere appendage of theological motivation? The Church is
tempted to strengthen and stabilize with higher authority both
her own structures and those of the state. An effective
change of structure in Church or state then threatens to reveal
its lack of credible theological foundation. A political ecclesiology would prefer to start from the notion of Church as the
anticipatory form of society's eschatological realization and
from her ability to renew society. 'Church' in this sense means
not the hierarchical magisterium but the living Church itself as
the community of the 'first free members of creation' (J. Moltmann).

7   Salvific apostolate of the Church[10]

The social aspects of salvation and of the eschatological horizon
of promise also affect the Church's salvific apostolate. L. Rütti
in *The Theology of Mission* has applied these various tendencies
and directions of theology to the practical field of missions and
developed a new concept.

The Church's salvific apostolate cannot ignore the social
nature of man in sin and salvation. In fact her prime function
is in that area. Unlike secular salvific movements and activities,
however, the Church approaches the world in the light of an
eschatological fulfilment. The promise of God's Kingdom in
Jesus discloses the world's redeemed and liberated future. The
eschatological perspective of salvation corresponds to a Christology which sees such a future founded and instituted by Jesus.
In order to avoid and correct all past attempts to narrow this
horizon of promise, Rütti deliberately names fewer components
of this salvation; he defines it rather from the point of view of
the world and of society.

Because the Church's apostolate directs the Church to her
proper field of operation, this extension and universality of the
purpose of mission involve also a change in her salvific apostolate and ecclesial structures. The world is the proper object of
that apostolate, which hopes to lead it to the fulfilment of the
promise made to it. Consequently every attempt to limit the
aims of mission to the Church's own survival and interests is
misconceived, for today neither personal conversion nor even

the building up the Church can be the purpose of the apostolate. Ecclesiocentrism has yielded pride of place to openness to the world. The recipient and the content of this apostolate is, again unlike the traditional concept of mission, the entire man as an individual *and* as a socially determined being, so that the political area cannot be excluded from mission. The eschatological horizon of promise sheds on the whole earthly reality the critical and transforming light of salvation that exceeds all existing circumstances. Mission cannot contribute to the conservation of existing circumstances by privatizing its purposes and ignoring wider issues. It must encourage the advent of eschatological *shalom*, from which the existing circumstances of unfreedom and manifold misery are still far distant. With his concept of *shalom* or Kingdom of God, Rütti intends to avoid the need to enumerate individual components of salvation, which was almost inevitable in a dualistic separation. And yet it remains a little obscure how human development and fulfilment on the one hand and God's eschatological revelation to man on the other relate to and condition each other. The critical denial of all dualism in both the objects of salvation and the apostolate is so much in the foreground of his thinking that he applies the blanket concepts and symbols as they stand, without analysing the various aspects they bring together—for example, the salvation of man in his elemental bodily existence, in his individuality and social context, in his worldliness and relation to God. This conjunction of concepts and missions of salvation, which had hitherto gone their own ways, inevitably affects the Church and her structures. If bodily and spiritual salvation are not to be separated in the apostolate of salvation—Rütti seems to think that difference entails separation—the apostolate is borne by the whole Church and every act of service of the individual Christian. Mission is not limited to verbal proclamation and evangelization. Assistance given to developing countries cannot either be excluded as of little importance or regarded as the main business. No, the Church's apostolate of salvation takes place only in the context of salvific wholeness. This new concept of the world's attentiveness and openness to its promised future has implications for the ecclesial structure which Rütti applies to the Church's ecumenical aspects, her

67

offices, her preaching, and so forth. And despite any reservations one might have, Rütti has at least outlined a global view of the new salvific apostolate.

7

Salvation
in the present and future:
soteriology and eschatology[1]

Recent developments in the theology of salvation cannot be explained as due solely to internal factors. Scrutiny of Christian tradition and its sources has been encouraged, primarily in soteriology, by common human experiences and dangers. As regards the social dimension of sin and salvation, the newly undertaken dialogue with Marxism has led both partners to a change of heart and a re-examination of positions hardened in polemic. In the long period of their mutual hostility Christian belief concerning redemption and Marxist materialism, in their most opposed forms, had hardly discussed matters of common social interest. The expectations both of the Christian and of the Marxist doctrine pointed in such apparently irreconcilable directions that their proponents never even met, much less engaged in fruitful dialogue. Dialogue became possible and prospered for two reasons. On the one side, Marxism recognized a difference between itself and its political embodiments, for example in the attitude of the various Marxist philosophers towards the brutal Soviet communism of Stalin; and on the other side, Christians came to recognize that their beliefs on the subject of redemption had failed to do justice to every aspect of human salvation. Marxism began seriously to consider a more personal humanism, while Christian soteriology turned its attention to social matters. Another factor fostering dialogue was common concern for the future, even though the two sides looked at it in very different ways. In several strides Christian theology had turned from a system of unhistorical theological categories to an understanding of the Bible based on salvation history and thence soon to a rediscovery of eschatology. This in its turn brought a stronger concentration of previously scattered eschatological statements. However, a common horizon of understanding, experience, and questioning of the future is the presupposition both of a genuine critical discussion and of a constructive communication and co-operation. The evolution of belief concerning salvation under the questioning and critical influence of Marxism therefore requires a chapter of its own.

1 *Critique of the common features of*
  soteriology and eschatology[2]

Two aspects are common to Christian soteriology and eschatology, and have therefore attracted the same criticism, which arose primarily in opposition to Marxism, but also became self-criticism on the part of theology. Those two aspects are the transcendence of salvation or of the absolute future, and the transcendence of the fulfilment of salvation or of the future. In both cases the reality and effectiveness of God seem to exclude other worldly and human activities, whereas it must be shown that this view rests on a misunderstanding.

Christians appeared to believe that man's true salvation and future fulfilment resulted not from finite human activity but from the operation of God. This distinction was understood in only one way, which excluded any possibility of intercourse with the world, due partly to the fact that God was located in a realm of spiritual, immaterial, eternal, and therefore suprahistorical reality. Man's salvation was thought to lie beyond the limits of his immediate experience of the world. It was associated linguistically with 'saving one's soul', with release from 'this vale of tears', with 'eternal salvation'. (Linguistic usage often betrays concepts even where the underlying theology might be accurate.) The future was similarly travestied: God alone could effect the infinite openness of man's spirit and freedom. The world, history, and man as a total, bodily being, all lost any claim to be 'last things'. The fact that the 'resurrection of the flesh'—an integral part of traditional belief—itself defied any attempt to limit the *eschata* to infinite, other-worldly realities was somehow lost sight of.

Logically, only God's own activity could lead to transcendent salvation and an absolute future thus conceived. Only God could communicate himself to man as salvation; only God could bring fulfilment if this consisted in blessed communion with him.

Because salvation and fulfilment were divine gifts not at man's disposal, there was no sense in asking what man could contribute by his own activity. The theory that human works meant something was dismissed as synergism or the heresy of self-saving and self-fulfilment. This lay behind the Christian critique of Marxism and other secularist doctrines of salvation. Attempts to save and fulfil oneself were replaced in polemic by salvation and fulfilment granted and effected solely by God. It made no very great difference whether this defamation of human struggle was perpetrated by the Roman Catholic understanding of grace and the sacramental communication of grace or by Luther's theory of justification by faith without works. At best there was in Catholic tradition, apart from Augustine's theology of grace, a sort of unsystematic Pelagianism, at least as regards securing the salvation of the individual. Salvation and fulfilment, however, were so much God's own work that they were not to be prejudiced by man's arrogant attempt to co-operate.

2 *From exclusive to inclusive eschatology*[3]

In theory, and perhaps earlier than the development of any such theory, the self-critical examination of this exclusiveness was prompted by Christian praxis. Not only did other statements in which concern for his salvation, the new way of life, and the new style of activity enjoined on man co-exist with those proclamations of God's absoluteness and the exclusiveness of his work; Christians struggled in happy inconsequence to serve the salvation of the whole man, and committed themselves to improving social conditions among the workers or developing nations. Such praxis was constantly redressing the imbalance of an exclusive soteriology and eschatology. It gave Christians an experiential certainty that could not be led astray by slogans proclaiming the all-sufficiency of God and his grace. The experience of total salvation had sooner or later to lead Christians to question these pious simplifications and to provide a proper theological and spiritual basis for itself. In the long term, no Christian whose experience had given him the certainties of total salvation could live with a theory that took so little notice of his experience.

71

Stimulated by this question, Christian eschatology turned its attention away from one or at the most a few symbols of salvific fulfilment, such as the beatific vision (itself a very one-sided concept), to the rich images of biblical promise in the Old and the New Testament: the promised land, the city of God's indwelling with his people, the banquet of the messianic age, the parables of the Kingdom, the general resurrection of the dead, the new heaven and new earth. Admittedly these images are so structured in the Bible that God always remains the means of fulfilment, but it is also true that God leads man and his world to fulfilment. The 'absolute future' could only be described as correlative, since these images, despite all their differences, exhibit a correlative structure by allowing God to be 'with us'. This future, therefore, could not be limited to the reality of the God who revealed and communicated himself, because this movement included those *to whom* he communicated himself and gave a share of his own life. *Of whom* is God the absolute future? The integrity of fulfilment again forced itself on Christian eschatology, not because of concessions and a bad conscience in the face of ideological pluralism, but from the heart of Christian promise and hope.

Similarly Christian eschatology could not be satisfied with dismissing other concepts of the future, other utopias, as relative to God's—and now man's—absolute future. That future, of course, exceeds and transcends every human and therefore finite plan for the future and its realization. The first witness of Christian eschatology, therefore, can and must be to de-ideologize totalitarian programmes for the future. It means a great deal for man to stay free in the face of the totalitarian claims of such programmes and deny them any pretence to be absolute. None the less, critical relativization cannot be the only relationship of the absolute future to these historical objectives. However difficult it may seem to determine the positive eschatological value of any particular historical goal, man's striving, his ethical self-realization, and his humanistic shaping of the world cannot be reduced to the external observance of the virtues or to a pilgrim's 'merit' on the way to the eternal reward. Just as in Jesus the tension between present and future characteristic of the Kingdom of God permits and offers a present inauguration of what lies fully only in the future, so human conduct must include a hidden initiatory or proleptic presence and realization. The statements in the New Testament about spiritual (and consequently new and eschatological) existence, and about man's corresponding need to change, confer an eschatological quality not only on this subjective activity but also on its external manifestations. These become the 'fruit of the Spirit' (Gal. 5.22), the 'fruit of light' (Eph. 5.9). The superimposition of present and future, which in the New Testament theology of history is based not on some abstract schema but on the reality of the Christ-event, is communicated to the believer's activity in the spiritual experience which appropriates it.

This demonstrates the inadequacy of the third limitation of salvation, the attempt to regard salvation and fulfilment as exclusively God's work and human 'works' as detracting from God's gracious activity. Even though theology has never succeeded in fully clarifying the relationship between human responsibility and divine grace, quietism and its opposite, a legalistic, activistic approach, can certainly be regarded as misconceptions. It is particularly striking that the divine promise is appealed to as a call to hope and renunciation of doubt, as an admonition to change and as a liberation of the old man. The *extra nos* of salvation, the new history between God and the world not initiated by man, shows man to be one who receives and listens, but his freedom is called to an *active* reception and listening. Justification by grace without works arouses in him the decision of faith. Correspondingly, the promise calls to active hope beyond all human possibilities. Fulfilment must come as part of a freely accepted covenant between God and man. There must be room for human freedom in the future opened up by God's promise. More than that, a responsibility not otherwise possible is expected of man, as is apparent in the symbolic image of fulfilment as a judgement.

We have seen that on three fronts eschatology has modified its stance. If the Marxist critique of religion has also given considerable impetus to this self-critique, the renewed eschatology still, of course, maintains God's transcendence and sovereign absoluteness, but it does so not at the expense of the human, secular, historical future, but in order to safeguard it.

3   *Marxist critique of religion and its christological differentiation*[4]

In the first decades of the Marxist critique of religion—apart from a few significant traces in Marx himself and others—religion in its historical, ecclesiastical form seemed to be only a hindrance to human and social liberation, a brake on the revolution. Religion gave the economic and political bosses the theocratic justification and stabilizing force of their authority. In its theology of creation, it stabilized the world and man ontocratically on authorities without enabling them to transcend their present. Theonomy was a definition of man which alienated him from himself, from the possibilities of his future and freedom, and referred him beyond himself to God. Finally, the Christian religion bestowed on suffering an immanent significance and a paradoxical value that were threatened by every attempt to relieve the suffering. But this readiness to suffer was for the benefit of those who had reason to fear that conquest of suffering and the abolition of slavery would imperil their rights of ownership. Not only Marxist but also Christian authors quote in this context Luther's remark to the peasants in revolt: 'Suffering is the Christian lot'. Their masters must have felt all the more secure and rejoiced accordingly. This overall Marxist judgement on religion makes an exception in the surprisingly intense Marxist preoccupation with Christianity and the person of Jesus of Nazareth. It excepts Jesus himself from religious misunderstandings and their consequences. The 'Jesus phenomenon' has been the object of assiduous Marxist interest which, for example in M. Machoveč's *A Marxist Looks at Jesus*,[5] is at pains to carry out a careful exegesis and has a high moral tone. In the life and teaching of Jesus, religion seems to have been a relationship with God which hastens, not delays, change. In this context, it is possible to view and practise religion not as a sedative—as the 'opium of the people'—but as an active protest against misery. Jesus's proclamation of the Kingdom of God resulted not in setting men's minds at rest but in shaking them out of their torpor. All existing power, and those who wielded it, were placed under the judgement and faced with a crisis. Herod's terror at the question of the wise men and Pilate's fear were alike symptoms of the unsettling presence and proximity of God's lordship. We cannot argue from Jesus's criticism of kingdoms and his consideration of the poor as 'blessed' to an evil or good inherent in these conditions, much less to a simple inversion of existing relationships; but at least the call to justice and conversion did not go out to an isolated soul or appeal for a spiritual attitude of poverty; it removed the security based on possession. The judgement condemning unjust mammon does not await the coming of some future world beyond the present: it is already delivered in this world, it concerns all human ownership now.

Above all, the proximity and presence of God's lordship displays a divine concern for man which excludes no dimension as unimportant, which seeks to free man from all experiences of slavery and death and bring him to the fullness of life. The synoptic combination of forgiveness of sin and healing, of expulsion of devils and physical recovery, does not, obviously, present a fully elaborated anthropology or soteriology, but the situations of healing chosen leave no doubt as to the wholeness and total presence of salvation for man. Again the fear that the religious appeal to God leaves man at a disadvantage is seen to be unfounded. If this is so, the concept and meaning of religion in social development must be re-defined, or else the relationship between the praxis of Jesus and his religious thinking is self-contradictory. Either a new concept of religion must be worked out, or the unity of Jesus and his relation to God must be broken and regarded as a religious residue not yet expunged. Machovec, and in our view Dorothee Sölle, choose yet another path. The religious elements in Jesus's language are interpreted as symbolic metaphors for the absoluteness of human values which it protects and realizes. The 'Kingdom of God' stands for man's new society, 'sonship of God' for man's new identity revealed by Jesus the representative. The nexus between forgiveness as first experienced and forgiveness as guaranteed in the future is dissolved and reduced to the postulate of forgiveness. The question is whether Jesus's experience and intention are here preserved.

4   *The tradition of a subversive Jesus as an alternative to the churches' tradition of Christ*[6]

In several aphoristic alternatives the Marxist 'christology' offers a new version of the churches' 'fall'. Formerly, the piety and theology of the Church were accused of divinizing the man Jesus under the influence of hellenism. Now they are accused of weakening and domesticating the dangerous and radical nature of Jesus's message and conduct. The primitive blunting of the gospel is pilloried in phrases such as 'Jesus the fire-raiser', 'Christ the fire-fighter'.[7] Paul, for example, turned the death of Jesus on the cross, which the synoptics interpreted as an attack on the law and on the reactions to Jesus's salvific ministry, into a stylized redemptive death with its own meaning and fruitfulness. He left the cross of Jesus and his suffering brothers in place; he even set it up again. He also reduced the consequences of the new freedom in Jesus Christ to a dialectical emancipation of the slave and enslavement of the free (1 Cor. 7.22), instead of working out the social implications of freedom for slaves. Unlike Jesus's eschatological ministry, Paul located social emancipation in a realm beyond history, without any imminent expectation of it.

To this prevailing, official Christ-tradition, which accompanied a dogmatic Christology, Ernst Bloch especially has opposed a latent and buried 'subversive Jesus-tradition' which he bases on Old and New Testament fragments that witness to man's amazing freedom and independence with regard to God. Jacob's struggle with the angel would be a case in point (Gen. 32.24). Another would be the serpent's promise that in eating the fruit of the forbidden tree man would be like God (Gen. 3.5). The Exodus is understood as the prototype and motive-force for the history of man's increasing liberation from slavery and heteronomy, until theonomy itself is defeated and repelled as just such a heteronomy. Bloch sees the climax of this 'promethean religion', which leads to the abolition of religion, in the dogmatic formulation of Nicaea, which declares the man Jesus consubstantial with God and so divinizes man, annulling the pre-eminence and superiority of God. With amazing erudition Bloch traces all the religious movements of Christianity which have embodied the social and revolutionary energy of the gospel: the poverty movements of the middle ages, the sixteenth-century Anabaptists, Religious Socialism, and other such phenomena. Unfortunately those movements were still insufficiently radical and critical to reject the religious foundations themselves which delayed the liberating advent of man as man-by-himself, as man in his not-yet-attained eschatological form.

Although much in this counter-Christology can be attributed to a biased selection and interpretation of data, it casts a critical eye on the attempts and temptations which lay in the development of ecclesial belief and were effective even where the indefinable authority of Jesus was not fossilized in religious titles and where the unsettling influence of his message was not made flabby by Christology.

5   Agreement and open questions[8]

Both parties in this dialogue—Christian eschatology and Marxist utopia—have emerged transformed and must have gained a more accurate nuanced picture of each other. Marxism can no longer be viewed as straightforward materialism or mere collectivist social theory. It too asks what is the moving force and the receding goal of humanity and society. It is thus *open to transcendence*, even though it cannot specify any particular transcendental reality. The threats to man from scientific and technical positivism, from consuming superficiality in economically rich countries, from poverty and dependence in the Third World, and also from state guardianship in communist states call together Marxists and Christians for the protection of humanity, freedom, and personality. Conversely, Christian eschatology and soteriology recognize the justice of Marxism's challenge, of the selfless ethos and, still more, of the risk which an original and impartial thought in totalitarian systems entails for Marxist philosophers and citizens. Without this impulse, the renewal of eschatology would be—and at first was—more a theological process which brought together scattered statements and aspects. Influenced by the Marxist challenge, it was forced to look for a new relevance. Meanwhile the question arises for the Christian understanding of salvation how, on this common basis, we are to think of and realize the uniqueness and shape of Christian hope and integral salvation. The temporary emphasis on what was previously neglected slightly obscures this task, but it allows us no delay in working out the *proprium christianum* in our understanding of salvation.

Here, then, remain a number of open questions which theology cannot sidestep if it is to be an honest partner in dialogue. They concern the ever-erupting self-transcendence of man and his achievements, the elusive inspiration and motivation of social change and its leading ideas. The mystery of death has always been and is still the touchstone of human utopias. It is accepted more honestly when it is endured in silence than when it is glossed over and belittled.

8

Present-day salvation praxis considered in relation to the origin and the completion of salvation[1]

In our brief review of recent reinterpretations in soteriology, the hermeneutical problem, particularly as a linguistic one, has been all-important. How has the original salvific message of Jesus been understood over the ages and incorporated into the varying contexts of man's experiences of sin and expectations of salvation? We have been aware that the linguistic problem includes the further substantial problems of the experience of salvation and of how salvation is realized in practice. So far, perhaps, we have been taking for granted something that must now be dealt with directly in this our final chapter. What is the precise relationship between the modern understanding and praxis of salvation and the original salvific event, which must be the basis and norm of Christian belief? And what is the relationship between them and the completion of salvation, which is to close and fulfil the present historical realization of salvation? In an age which took for granted the relationship of the present to the past and future, the problem was not acute. Nor did it impinge on an understanding of salvation which had no clear awareness of salvation as an event and as history, as regards either its present or its origin and fulfilment. Between these two extremes, however, man's present awareness of and feel for history appear to be something we can safely assume; the present is sufficiently cognisant of history to see the difference, and is yet not so rooted in history that it thinks that its historical roots pose no problems.

The problem, consequently, is of more than theoretical interest, because the three corners of our triangle—the past, the present, and the future of salvation as history and event—have been stressed in different ways and give rise to three different lines of thought.

1 Centres of gravity in the history of salvation[2]

The traditional understanding of redemption concentrates its soteriology almost exclusively on the redemptive work of Jesus, the salvific significance of his life, death, and resurrection. These events enshrine what has come to be called 'objective' redemption, which has then merely to be communicated to the individual in the subsequent course of history. This communication is usually treated somewhere other than in soteriology: in ecclesiology, sacramentology, and of course moral theology. This exclusiveness of the redemptive event seems to be based on and demanded by its universal significance. The historical uniqueness and definitiveness express salvation's *extra nos*, to which all the rest of secular time is directed. The result of this approach is to stunt the effect and influence of redemption, which, at most, becomes the application and appropriation of the salvific event.

In the opposite direction lies an understanding of redemption which, because of God's present hiddenness and man's repeated experience of weakness, places all its hope on a future revelation and realization of salvation. Several strands of New Testament soteriology have led to this change of emphasis. The New Testament looks forward to the realization of salvation as an outstanding and non-disposable future, which must not be anticipated by an attempt to effect salvation by force and prematurely. One result of this renewed emphasis on the virtue of hope has been the rejection of a fanatical or triumphalistic assurance of salvation. Especially where the Church has thought of herself as the Kingdom of God already established, the paradoxical hiddenness of justification and of man's new life, despite his sinfulness and mortality, has been recalled. So firmly has the future been believed to be the only period of time to which salvation should be referred, that one feels obliged in face of this conviction to question the role of the past event of salvation and its possibility here and now. This leads us to the third view of soteriology. The *present* realization of salvation coincides with a stressing of human responsibility and active belief. The salvific event achieved in Jesus Christ gains significance on this understanding only in so far as it is accepted and actively

80

appropriated in present belief. Future salvation must not merely be hoped for as a future event; it must reach back through present symbolic salvific activity into the present. This verification of history and the future in present realization not only characterizes our understanding of soteriology but also determines the style of the rest of our theology. Suspicion of an objectifying discourse on God which is not situated in the context of the believing subject; the existential interpretation of traditional kerygma; the anthropological 'repatriation' (if we may thus avoid the negative word 'reduction') of christological and eschatological statements: all these relate to the subject. The interpretation of tradition and the significance of history are determined by the subject. The impression can, but should not, arise that the appropriation of the salvific event in faith and our existential interpretation constitute and found the existence and full significance of God, and of Jesus Christ, his history and his future. It is surely true that past and future history are objectified in the bad sense if they are not 'made present' to us.

These variations in ways of conceiving the three points of the historical progression of salvation constitute the main problem of soteriology. How was and is this tension experienced and sustained; but above all, how mastered and solved? Tradition and present-day theology have different categories of mediation for this, which can be grouped as christological, ecclesiological, and pneumatological; nor are those types mutually exclusive.

2 *Christological mediation*[3]

What is the significance of Jesus's life and history for the present realization of salvation? Where this is not simply taken for granted and accepted as a truth of faith, theology has drawn on several models of mediation which are intended to bind together Jesus's past history and the believer's own present.

The concept of representation or substitution is suggested by the anthropology of the Old and the New Testament, as well as by many traditions known to the history of culture. The acts of one person can stand for those of another and be accepted as his. If this concept and its frequent biblical use are less accessible to us today—for example in the eucharistic formula 'for you'—it is because the concept of representation no longer carries for us the connotations it once did. Representation is dismissed as a merely external, juridical attribution, only where the individual is regarded as a historically isolated figure. For 'substitution' to be possible, there must be a common history, national or human, between the representative and those represented. This common history is expressed, for example, by the symbolic names of incorporated realities which express at one and the same time the individual member of a nation, family, or royal house *and* a collectivity: Adam, Jacob, Israel; but also Body of Christ, Son of Man, the new Adam, and so on. In this incorporation the common bond and solidarity of the individual members becomes intelligible without, however, merging and absorbing the individual into an anonymous collectivity. The historical distance between primitive and modern salvation, therefore, presents no particular problem, because individual events cannot be isolated in an individual's history alone, but always partake of a wider context of exchange and mutual influence.

Corporative solidarity and historical intercommunication pose a problem, and are therefore understood with difficulty, only when the individual is regarded as a responsible and juridical subject in his own right before God. In connection with the medieval theory of satisfaction, the 'transfer' of salvation from Christ to the believer was accomplished with the juridical category of merit. Christ's satisfaction achieved an excess of merit in which other people, including those who come after him, can share. The historical distance could be more easily overcome in so far as the real correlative reality of man in his quest for salvation was not Jesus Christ but the eternal, supratemporal, and also therefore contemporary God. God's forgiveness was the grace of *Christ* only to the extent that it was effected and made possible once for all by the merit of his death. Merit and grace could be detached from the meriting person and from the meritorious, salvific event, and so more easily be borne by history. The original event lingered on in grateful memory—but in memory none the less.

Mediation was even easier when Jesus Christ was accorded the supreme significance of exemplary life and action to which the 'imitation of Christ' was oriented, whether in personal and interior sanctification or, in an extended sense, in human living as a whole. In this case the historical distance was acknowledged, but it was thought it could be bridged by Jesus's exemplary action (which could be made present and effective for salvation only as an example to man). The believer and disciple, however, received on this conception no more than moral teaching and a persuasive model. In implementing that teaching, he was dependent on his own resources, which allowed him a love or hope just as persuasive as they were proper to Jesus. In this mediation, the significance not only of history but also of the person of Jesus diminished: ultimately, mediated salvation could be detached from the person and presence of Jesus.

A more satisfactory way of bridging the historical gap is suggested by a specifically christological possibility, which arises from the eschatological quality of the event and reality of the resurrection. The event of Easter does not lie in linear continuity with Jesus's earthly history, but affects our history tangentially by adding a qualitatively new dimension of time. As the one risen from the dead, Jesus does not simply perpetuate his earthly existence, but stands in an immediate relationship of *presence* to every age. At the same time his *historical* life is preserved in his paschal existence: the crucified one is the risen one, and vice versa. By virtue of this history, preserved in his person, the relation between the person, work, significance, and efficacy of Jesus is retained without any need to introduce mediating categories such as merit. The relationship of 'objective' redemption achieved by the historical Jesus to 'subjective' redemption as evinced in man's continuing appropriation and realization of salvation is then concentrated in the person of the risen and glorified Lord. The history on which salvation is based does not therefore remain in the past, but continually reaches forward into the present. Nevertheless, the difficulty of this mediation consists in the fact that it shatters the conceptual models of man's situation in time and history by opening up a qualitatively new dimension of time. We can understand this new dimension only negatively and periphrastically; our only grasp on it is the similar experience of the disciples when the risen one revealed himself to them.

3   *Ecclesiological mediation*[4]

From earliest times the Church, in whom, by her creed, by her witness in life and preaching, and by her saving sacraments men carry salvation through history, has acted as a medium between the salvific events of the past and those of the future. If we now briefly develop these forms whereby the Church has mediated salvation, the foregoing christological mediation does not suddenly become superfluous. No mediation by the Church could of itself confer a historical meaning and presence on the life of Jesus unless it were first his own and enjoined by him on the Church. The forms of mediation employed by the Church therefore presuppose, temporally and objectively, the universal, historical significance of the Christ-event, and can only testify to this significance, not constitute it. Nevertheless, on this presupposition an indispensable significance accrues to the Church and her ministry of salvation. Trying to do without human witness to salvation would be merely a supernaturalistic pretext for avoiding responsibility.

The recent critical extension of salvation and the emphasis on salvation's total human content has also led to an extension of the Church's witness to salvation. We can see it, for example, in the fact that prior to all fragmentation into individual services the entire people of God is responsible for the salvific mission, whatever forms that service may take in the lives of individual members. We can see it also in the fact that salvation is again considered to be extended to man not only linguistically in the Church's creed, preaching, and liturgy, but also existentially in the experiences and encounters of belief and love wherever these occur in and between people. Such experiences are 'unofficial' and cannot be systematized. If we are to speak of an express salvific witness and service of the Church, it must be incorporated into this wider context, whether there be question of preaching, counselling, helps to belief, community pastoral care, or whatever. We must not here make a facile distinction, concerning ourselves in some cases with bodily, secular salvation and in others with spiritual, eternal salvation. Where there is question of the salvation of man, of that being who experiences himself in his personal and therefore also eternal existence

84

as a bodily, secular being, there can be no justification for separating out two parallel strands of wholeness (whatever that might mean).

A differentiation of particular services becomes possible and necessary only within this overall salvific apostolate. The linguistic witness to salvation in Jesus Christ is not an additional, and therefore dispensable, label affixed to a salvation which is also pre-linguistic and implicit ('anonymous'); it alone restores the unequivocal, primordial relationship to Jesus Christ, whose person and history are vital to salvation and are its foundation. If he, as a historical figure, opens up the possibility of new humanity, that possibility cannot be offered without historical, explicit witness. Language is not a form of human communication which is added to reality and experience: reality comes to itself only in human communication.

The proper significance of liturgical celebration as a symbolic witness to and mediation of salvation has been temporarily obscured by the urgency and complexity of particular ecclesial and social issues. Celebration of the Eucharist, regarded by some as 'pointless', achieves its proper justification and significance where there is considered reflection on origin and fulfilment. Human activity can move on only one level of awareness at any given time, there is no need for all references to source and meaning to be consciously maintained in the enactment. On the other hand, human activity is dependent on reflection, on the linguistic and symbolic presentation of all these past and future references: on the origin and goal of love and hope. Similarly the community cannot maintain its common posture of faith only by living it; it must recall and confirm it in celebration. The eucharistic celebration enables the Church to experience in her witness to salvation the source of her mission and authority, so that in the celebration she can again allow this source to be bestowed on her. The Eucharist also broadens the Church's horizon and gives her a foretaste of the goal of her history and salvific witness. In the joy of the shared table, the consummation is not merely placed before and enjoined on her as a legal obligation, but is also granted proleptically as an inspiriting promise. Rightly understood, the reference to salvation as an event in the past and consideration of the consummation of sal-

85

vation in the future are not appended to a self-explanatory salvific praxis; such praxis needs, as an integral component of its present, the source that revitalizes and the promise that attracts. Time set aside for the eucharistic celebration is not lost to the urgent effort of salvation. On the contrary, only then can that effort serve salvation in faith and hope.

Symptomatic of the opposing modern opinions on liturgical celebration as part of the Church's salvific apostolate are two books by Harvey Cox,[5] who in the first pleaded for the 'secular city' and excluded 'sacral' activities and areas, but soon afterwards, in the *Feast of Fools*, considered feasting and festivity essential if man is not to narrow his horizons.

4 *Pneumatological mediation*[6]

The New Testament suggests pneumatology, not as a third category of mediation over and above the christological and ecclesiological ones, but as one that stands in a mutual relation of ordination and interpenetration. It has therefore been increasingly studied in close conjunction with recent Christology and soteriology. Nevertheless, the recent revival of interest in experiences of the Spirit still fails to do full justice to the complexity of salvific praxis, because it tends to limit itself to the individual and social experience of the Spirit's presence.

New Testament pneumatology includes an answer to the problem of mediation between the event and praxis of salvation in so far as it spans and holds together the dialectic of Jesus's historical and personal uniqueness. The Spirit of Jesus keeps the origin of his person and history, message and ministry alive in our minds, but that Spirit can also break out of the rigid historical framework and enable Christ himself to be present. This possibility, of course, rests on the resurrection and ascension of Jesus, as man's experience of the Spirit testifies to the risen Jesus; pneuma is the dynamic presence of the crucified and risen Christ. At the same time the Spirit participates in God's new eschatological reality which the risen one has entered. To the extent that the Spirit leaves history and enters the present, he also breaks out of the future into the present and witnesses to the future not only in word or promise, but also in a real foretaste of glorification. In terms of Christology, it means that he brings into the present both Christ's history and Christ's return. Christology, thus transformed into pneumatology, enables us to join together the three areas of time which it both holds together and separates from each other in their uniqueness. This it now achieves, however, not by dispensing objective salvific realities such as grace, merit, and example, but by making Christ's person present in the Spirit.

It would be over-enthusiastic to imagine that the ecclesiological making-present in human, historical activity, tradition, witness, and proclamation are made superfluous by the pneumatological category of mediation. The New Testament sees the witness of the Spirit and the human witness of the Church not as competitors but as two currents that conjoin, each making the other possible: 'But when the Counsellor comes, whom I shall send to you from the Father, even the Spirit of truth ... he will bear witness to me; and you also are witnesses, because you have been with me from the beginning' (John 15.26–7). The witness of the Church can bring Christ's message and ministry into our present as living things only if it is sustained by the continuing presence of the Spirit. Conversely, the Spirit's witness is embodied—achieves concrete form and presence—in the Church's witness. Of itself the Church's mediation of salvation does not measure up to the salvific event, because it cannot control Christ's free presence. The Church's need of the Spirit rests not only on her creaturely finitude and sinful insufficiency for salvation, but also on the peculiarity of Christian salvation, which is not to be separated either in its origin or in its daily appropriation from the Person and life of Jesus. Now, however, the Church can—and must— understand human witness and activity as a salvific presence, provided only that it has been kindled and animated by the Spirit. After a phase in which Christian salvific praxis has drawn nearer theoretically, linguistically, and practically, to modern secular efforts to humanize and liberate, it is not inopportune to recall the imbalance between human action and God's salvific work. In the context of secular expectations of salvation, the peculiarity of Christian salvation must be expressed not only theoretically with the categories of 'absolute future' and 'indisposable source'; with an express reference and openness to

87

the Spirit, Christians must experience the Spirit and the continuity of salvation he establishes.

In the Christian service of salvation, preaching, diaconal effort, and social commitment come up against both the limits of human success, where the question of satisfying man's infinity is at its most crucial, and the limits of human failure. Even in itself, however, Christian witness to salvation is subject to the same limits: hope it cannot summon, strength it cannot find. Nevertheless, not only at these limits, where our ability ends, but long before, within our very ability, Christian witness to salvation knows, conceptually and experientially, that it is moved by the command and life of the risen Lord—by the Spirit who raises from the dead not Jesus alone but man and the world along with him.

Conclusion

Soteriology as the preservation of faith's reality

This rapid survey of different concepts of soteriology, which have been adopted, criticized, or modified in various recent interpretations, is far from complete. The theological elaboration of the question of salvation in areas where man's salvation is threatened, and where neglected duties still await the attention of salvific praxis, is likewise also incomplete. A 'concretisation of redemption' with, among others, psychoanalytical and psychotherapeutical methods, should therefore be undertaken not only in the well-studied field of social change, but also in the neglected area of man's spiritual perils. The advances already made in pastoral praxis and practical theology need to be theologically grounded. The outstanding tasks, however, merely confirm that soteriology is precisely the field of theology in which the latter needs most acutely to be relevant.[1] Soteriology could aptly be described as theology's pace-maker. It shows that relevance cannot be looked for only in *practical* theology—at some stage, that is, *after* systematic theology—but in soteriology affects the heart of systematic theology itself.

Theology is required to approach the constantly changing human and social reality for the sake of greater intelligibility, so that it can enter man's horizon of understanding and area of experience. Soteriology also shows that the gap, not only between traditional and modern *language*, but more so between the original salvific event and its modern appropriation, in other words between historical and modern salvific *praxis*, needs to be bridged hermeneutically. If this hermeneutic is not undertaken, the message of salvation suffers not only from unintelligibility but also and more calamitously from ineffectiveness and meaninglessness. This book has tried to show that the Church's theology and praxis must alter their stance and approach the ever-changing human reality because of new experiences, in particular new experiences of sin, and expectations of salvation. The gap, the considerable difference in points of view, is detected most clearly in soteriology. Man's search for salvation and the Church's testimony to salvation no longer, alas, coincide. Fortunately, the soteriological praxis of Christians is more versatile and fast-moving than the theory. The Church's service of salvation, however, must not remain long without the critical but also inspiriting and encouraging orientation of theoretical soteriology. A soteriological position long abandoned and vacated by praxis becomes as unreal as a hospital in a depopulated territory.

It has transpired, from our examination of its many implications for other thematic areas of systematic theology, that soteriology has proved to be a continuous transcendental dimension and realignment of theology not limited to any particular field. Sooner or later soteriology affects the doctrine of God in his relation to creation and history. It can thus open even the closed circle of the life of the Trinity to Calvary, and also to man's sinfulness and new existence. We have also seen similar effects in ecclesiology and the sacramental system of the Church. Above all, soteriology has necessitated a complete rewriting of Christology. The objection that this makes Christology indistinguishable from the prevailing anthropology or social theory is not to be lightly brushed aside. It cannot, however, dispense us from taking the risk. To do so is better than alluring Christology or ecclesiology to retain their traditional identity at the cost of soteriological relevance. Not only Christology and ecclesiology, but also faith itself find their 'soul' not in keeping their distance, but in approaching man's ever new search for salvation. Christology's and ecclesiology's critique of action—which does not mean forcing themselves on human activity, but a constructive partnership—must and should take place in unflinching confrontation with the quest for salvation, in co-operation with other efforts to achieve a more human society. What salvation means for man at any given period cannot be deduced from his situation; it emerges only in the light

90

of the new man and the new human society in Jesus Christ. This reveals a factor unique to the Christian understanding of salvation. The new potentialities of man and society do not soar unattainably over man's finite potentialities, but awaken him from the death of his limitation and impotence. Bringing man from alienation to identity is not a service of the law, which leads to death and remains in death, but a service of the Spirit, who gives life. Even in this truth praxis frequently precedes theory. But what many anonymous Christians have already frequently experienced in the service of love and hope, and what has already proved to be a living truth to dead reality, must also become a theme of Christian soteriology. Relevance is then reversed: reality first calls theology to the truth; and then in its service to salvation it is faith which brings reality to the truth.

Notes

CHAPTER 1

Experiencing and bridging the gap between ourselves and traditional soteriology

1   Cf. A. T. Peperzak, *Der heutige Mensch und die Heilsfrage. Eine philosophische Hinführung*, Freiburg im Breisgau, 1972, pp. 9–78; G. Ebeling, 'Hermeneutische Theologie?', in *Wort und Glaube* II, Tübingen, 1969, pp. 99–120. (Only the first volume of this work, dating from 1960, has been translated into English: *Word and Faith*, London, 1963).

2   Cf. L. Scheffczyk, 'Die Aufgabe der Theologie angesichts der heutigen Erlösungsproblematik', in L. Scheffczyk (ed.), *Erlösung und Emanzipation* (Quaest. Disp. 61), Freiburg im Breisgau, 1973, pp. 5–12. The shift in the understanding of salvation has been verified not only in systematic theology but also in Church events. Cf. P. A. Potter (ed.), *Das Heil der Welt heute. Ende oder Beginn der Weltmission? Dokumente der Weltmissionskonferenz*, Bangkok 1973, Stuttgart, 1973.

3   For the historical relativity of soteriology and soteriological problems, cf. W. Pannenberg, *Grundzüge der Christologie*, Gütersloh, 1966², pp. 33–44.

4   Cf. G. Ebeling, 'Das Verständnis von Heil in säkularisierter Zeit', in *Wort und Glaube* III, Tübingen, 1975, pp. 349–61; K. Lehmann, 'Prolegomena zur theologischen Bewältigung der Säkularisierungsproblematik', in *Gegenwart des Glaubens*, Mainz, 1974, pp. 94–108; K. Rahner, 'Theological reflections on the problem of secularisation', in *Theol. Investig.* X, Part 4, New York and London, 1973, pp. 318–48; D. Sölle, *Christ the Representative. An Essay in Theology after the 'Death of God'*, London, 1967.

5   Cf. D. Bonhoeffer, *Widerstand und Ergebung*, new ed., Munich, 1970, pp. 376–80. (This new ed. contains material not in the first edition from which the ET was made: *Letters and Papers from Prison*, London, 1953, 1969. But cf. pp. 122–5.)

6   Cf. G. Ebeling, *Studium der Theologie. Eine enzyklopädische Orientierung*, Tübingen, 1975, esp. chap. 9: 'Praktische Theologie', pp. 113–29, and chap. 12: 'Fundamentaltheologie', pp. 162–75; W. Pannenberg, *Glaube und Wirklichkeit*, Munich, 1975, 'Wie wahr ist das Reden von Gott? Die wissenschaftstheoretische Problematik theologischer Aussagen', in *Grundlagen der Theologie. Ein Diskurs*, Stuttgart, 1974, pp. 29–41.

CHAPTER 2
A soteriologally guided re-examination
of the biblical sources

[1] For fundamental material here, see W. Foerster, article *sōzō*, in *Theol. Dict. of the NT* (Kittel), Grand Rapids, 1971, pp. 965–1025.

[2] Cf. N. Lohfink, 'Heil als Befreiung in Israel', in L. Scheffczyk (ed.), *Erlösung und Emanzipation* (see ch. 1 note 2), pp. 30–50.

[3] D. Bonhoeffer, *Widerstand und Ergebung* (see ch. 1 note 5), pp. 368f, 406f.

[4] This interpretation is proposed by E. Bloch, *Atheismus im Christentum. Zur Religion des Exodus und des Reichs*, Reinbek bei Hamburg, 1970, pp. 79–118.

[5] N. Lohfink, loc. cit (note 2 above), 32.

[6] Cf. H. H. Schmid, *sâlôm. 'Frieden' im Alten Orient und im Alten Testament*, Stuttgart, 1971, *Frieden ohne Illusionen. Die Bedeutung des Begriffs schalom als Grundlage für eine Theologie des Friedens*, Zurich, 1971. (The latter book is a shorter version of the former.)

[7] Cf. W. Eichrodt, *Theology of the Old Testament* I, London, 1961, esp. 'Fulfilling the Covenant: The Consummation of God's Dominion', pp. 472–511.

[8] Cf. G. von Rad, *Old Testament Theology* II (The Theology of Israel's Prophetic Traditions), Edinburgh, 1965, 1970, Part 3, chap. D, pp. 388–409: 'The Law'; H. Schmidt, *Frieden*, Stuttgart, 1969, esp. pp. 77–122: 'Schalom—die unwiderrufliche Provokation'.

[9] Cf. W. Zimmerli, *Der Mensch und seine Hoffnung im Alten Testament*, Göttingen, 1968.

[10] Cf. N. Lohfink, loc. cit. (note 2 above), p. 48.

[11] Cf. H. Kessler, *Erlösung als Befreiung*, Düsseldorf, 1972.

[12] Cf. H. Kessler, op. cit. (note 11), pp. 54–60.

[13] Cf. F. Mussner, *Die Wunder Jesu*, Munich, 1967; R. Pesch, *Jesu ureigene Taten? Ein Beitrag zur Wunderfrage* (Quaest. Disp. 52), Freiburg im Breisgau, 1970.

[14] Cf. E. Jüngel, *Paulus und Jesus*, Tübingen, 1967³, esp. pp. 87–215: 'Jesus und die Gottesherrschaft'.

[15] H. Kessler, op. cit. (note 1), pp. 17–25.

[16] H. Kessler, ibid., pp. 61–95, esp. 78–84: 'Der durch Jesus erschlossene Gott'.

[17] Cf. the two contributions of H. Kessler to the debate started by his article 'Erlösung als Befreiung? Zu einer Kontroverse,' in *Stimmen der Zeit* 191/12

(1973), pp. 849–53, and 'Erlösung als Befreiung?', ibid. 192/1 (1974), pp. 3–16.

¹⁸ Cf. F. Mussner, 'Ursprünge und Entfalung der neutestamentlichen Sohneschristologie. Versuch einer Rekonstruktion', in L. Scheffczyk (ed.), *Grundfragen der Christologie heute* (Quaest. Disp. 72), Freiburg im Breisgau, 1975, pp. 77–113.

CHAPTER 3

Death and resurrection of Jesus as a salvific event

¹ Cf. H. Kessler, *Die theologische Bedeutung des Todes Jesu. Eine traditionsgeschichtliche Untersuchung*, Düsseldorf, 1970, esp. pp. 228–329: 'Deutungen des Todes Jesu im Neuen Testament'; K. Kitamori, *Theologie des Schmerzes Gottes*, Göttingen, 1972.

² Cf. H. Kessler, *Erlösung als Befreiung*, Düsseldorf, 1972, esp. pp. 17–25; J. Moltmann, *The Crucified God. The Cross of Christ as the Foundation and Criticism of Christian Theology*, London, 1974, esp. pp. 126–59: 'Jesus' Way to the Cross'.

³ H. Kessler, op. cit. (preceding note). pp. 11–17, also criticizes it from the point of view of the history of traditions. In H. Schürmann, *Jesu ureigener Tod. Exegetische Besinnungen und Ausblick*, Freiburg im Breisgau, 1975, esp. pp. 66–96, the author considers the soteriological content of the words of institution.

⁴ Cf. K. Rahner, 'On the Theology of Death', in A. R. Caponigri (ed.), *Modern Catholic Thinkers* I, London, 1965, pp. 138–76; 'Theological Considerations concerning the Moment of Death', *Theol. Investig.* XI, Part 3, London, 1974, pp. 309–21.

⁵ Cf. L. Boros, *The Moment of Truth. Mysterium Mortis*, London, 1965.

⁶ Cf. E. Jüngel, *Tod*, Stuttgart, 1971, 'Vom Tod des lebendigen Gottes. Ein Plakat', in *Unterwegs zur Sache*, Munich, 1972, pp. 105–25.

⁷ H. U. von Balthasar, 'Mysterium Paschale', in *Mysterium Salutis* III/2, Einsiedeln, 1969, pp. 133–326 (French trans. Vol. 9, pp. 13–275), 'Abstieg zur Hölle', in *Pneuma und Institution. Skizzen zur Theologie* IV, Einsiedeln, 1974, pp. 387–400. (Only the first volume of the *Skizzen* has been translated into English: *Word and Revelation* and *Word and Redemption*, New York, 1964 and 1965 respectively.)

⁸ J. Moltmann, op. cit. (note 2 above), pp. 235–49: 'Trinitarian Theology of the Cross'.

⁹ Cf. D. Sölle, *Suffering*, Philadelphia, 1975.

¹⁰ Cf. U. Hedinger, *Wider die Versöhnung Gottes mit dem Elend. Eine Kritik des christlichen Theismus und A-Theismus*, Zurich, 1972; D. Wiederkehr, *Perspek-*

tiven der Eschatologie, Einsiedeln, 1974, esp. pp. 53–5 and 175f: 'Vom richtigen Gebrauch der Kreuz-rede und des Kreuz-motivs'.

[11] Cf. J. Moltmann, 'God and Resurrection', in *Hope and Planning*, London, 1971, pp. 31–55; W. Pannenberg, *Grundzüge der Christologie*, Gütersloh, 1966², esp. pp. 47–112, 'Dogmatische Erwägungen zur Auferstehung Jesu', in *Kerygma und Dogma* 14 (1968), pp. 105–18; K. Rahner and W. Thüsing, *Christologie—systematisch und exegetisch* (Quaest. Disp. 55), Freiburg im Breisgau, 1972, pp. 35–50 (K. Rahner), 123–32 (W. Thüsing).

CHAPTER 4
A critical analysis and reinterpretation of soteriological tradition

[1] Cf. G. Greshake, 'Der Wandel der Erlösungsvorstellungen in der Theologiegeschichte', in L. Scheffczyk (ed.), *Erlösung und Emanzipation* (see note 2), pp. 69–101; J. Plagnieux. *Heil und Heiland. Dogmengeschichtliche Texte und Studien*, Paris, 1969.

[2] Cf. A. Grillmeier, *Christ in Christian Tradition. From the apostolic age to Chalcedon (451)*, London, 1975², esp. pp. 153–487, *Mit ihm und in ihm. Christologie Forschungen und Perspektiven*, Freiburg im Breisgau, 1975, esp. pp. 421–582: 'Hermeneutik und Christologie'; W. Pannenberg, op. cit. (ch. 2. note 11), pp. 33–5: 'Vergottung durch Inkarnation und durch Angleichung an Gott', 'The Christological Foundation of Christian Anthropology', in *Concilium* 6, No. 9, June 1973 (Humanism in Question), pp. 86–100.

[3] Cf. G. Greshake, loc. cit. (note 1 above), pp. 83–94, 'Redemption and freedom', in *Theol. Dig.* 25 (1977), pp. 61–5; F. Hammer, *Genugtuung und Heil. Sinn und Grenzen der Erlösungslehre Anselms von Canterbury*, Vienna, 1967; R. Haubst, 'Anselms Satisfaktionslehre einst und heute', in *Trier Theol. Zeitscher*, 80 (1971), pp. 88–109; H. Kessler, op. cit. (ch. 3 note 1), esp. pp. 83–165.

[4] Cf. J. M. Lochmann, *Das radikale Erbe. Versuche theologischer Orientierung in Ost und West*, Zurich, 1972, esp. pp. 161–71: 'Das Erbe der Väter: Theologische Akzente der Böhmischen Reformation'; R. van Dülmen, *Das Täuferreich zu Münster 1534–1535. Berichte und Dokumente*, Munich, 1974. For the significance of the doctrine of the two kingdoms for social activity, cf. H.-H. Schrey (ed.), *Reich Gottes und Welt. Die Lehre Luthers von den zwei Reichen*, Darmstadt, 1969. See also K. H. Hertz (ed.), *Two Kingdoms and one world: a sourcebook in Christian social ethics*, Minneapolis, 1976.

⁵ G. Wehr (ed.), *Thomas Müntzer. Schriften und Briefe*, Frankfurt am Main, 1973, p. 97.

⁶ E. Bloch, *Thomas Müntzer als Theologe der Revolution*, Frankfurt am Main, 1963.

⁷ Cf. R. Breipohl (ed.), *Dokumente zum religiösen Sozialismus in Deutschland*, Munich, 1972; A. Lindt, *Leonhard Ragaz. Eine Studie zur Geschichte und Theologie des religiösen Sozialismus*, Zurich, 1957; M. Mattmüller, *Leonhard Ragaz. Eine Biographie* (two vols.), Zurich, 1957/68; P. Tillich, *Christentum und soziale Gestaltung. Frühe Schriften zum Religiösen Sozialismus*, Stuttgart, 1962; H.-H. Schrey, 'Sozialismus, Religiöser', in *Religion in Geschichte und Gegenwart* VI, pp. 181–6.

⁸ L. Ragaz, *Die Bergpredigt Jesu*, Hamburg, 1971, p. 7, cf. *Von Christus zu Marx—von Marx zu Christus*, Hamburg, 1972, *Die Gleichnisse Jesu. Seine soziale Botschaft*, Hamburg, 1971.

CHAPTER 5
Redemption in the context of man's search for meaning

¹ Cf. H. U. von Balthasar, *Die Gottesfrage des heutigen Menschen*, Vienna, 1956, 'Wer ist der Mensch?', in *Pneuma und Institution. Skizzen zur Theologie* IV (see remark in ch. 3 note 7), Einsiedeln, 1974, pp. 13–25; H. Gollwitzer, *Krummes Holz—Aufrechter Gang. Zur Frage nach dem Sinn des Lebens*, Munich, 1970, *Ich frage nach dem Sinn des Lebens*, Munich, 1974²; W. Pannenberg, *Was ist der Mensch? Die Anthropologie der Gegenwart im Lichte der Theologie*, Göttingen, 1962.

² Cf. K. Rahner, 'The "Commandment" of love in relation to the other commandments', in *Theol. Investig.* V, Baltimore and London, 1966, pp. 439–59, 'Reflections on the unity of the love of neighbour and the love of God', ibid. VI, Baltimore and London, 1969, pp. 231–49.

³ Cf. R. Affemann, 'Sünde und Erlösung in tiefenpsychologischer Sicht', in L. Scheffczyk (ed.), *Erlösung und Emanzipation* (ch. 1 note 2), pp. 15–29; H. Barz, *Selbst-Erfahrung. Tiefenpsychologie und christlicher Glaube*, Stuttgart, 1973; P. L. Berger, *A Rumour of Angels. Modern Society and the Rediscovery of the Supernatural*, Harmondsworth, 1970; G. Ebeling, 'Lebensangst und Glaubensanfechtung. Erwägungen zum Verhältnis von Psychotherapie und Theologie', in *Wort und Glaube* III, Tübingen, 1975, pp. 362–87; J. Moltmann, *Man. Christian Anthropology in the Conflicts of the Present*, Philadelphia, 1974, *The Crucified God* (see ch. 3 note 2), esp. pp. 291–316: 'Ways towards the Psychological Liberation of Man'; H. Müller-Pozzi, *Psychologie des Glaubens. Versuch einer Verhältnisbestimmung von Theologie und Psychologie*, Munich, 1975; K. Rahner, 'Guilt and its remission: the borderland between theology and psychotherapy', in *Theol. Investig.* II,

Baltimore and London, 1963, 1967, pp. 265–81, 'Guilt-Responsibility-Punishment within the view of Catholic theology', ibid. VI, Baltimore and London, 1969, pp. 197–217.

4   Cf. K. Rahner, 'Atheism and implicit Christianity', *Theol. Investig.* IX/2, New York and London, 1972, pp. 145–64, 'Christian humanism', ibid. IX/3, New York and London, 1972, pp. 187–204, 'The experience of God today', ibid. XI/2, New York and London, 1974, pp. 149–65, 'The quest for approaches leading to an understanding of the mystery of the God-Man Jesus', ibid. XIII/3, New York and London, 1975, pp. 195–200, 'Anonymer und expliziter Glaube', in *Schriften zur Theologie* XII, Einsiedeln, 1975, pp. 76–84; E. Klinger (ed.), *Christentum innerhalb und auberhalb der Kirche* (Quaest. Disp. 73), Frieburg im Breisgau, 1976.

5   Apart from the works mentioned in note 2, cf. K. Rahner, *Ich glaube an Jesus Christus*, Einsiedeln, 1968.

6   H. Braun, *Jesus. Der Mann aus Nazareth und seine Zeit*, Stuttgart, 1969², esp. pp. 159–70: 'Gott', 'Der Sinn der neutestamentlichen Christologie', in *Gesammelte Studien zum Neuen Testament und seiner Umwelt*, Tübingen, 1967², pp. 243–82, 'Die Problematik einer Theologie des Neuen Testaments', ibid., pp. 325–41.

7   Cf. W.-D. Marsch, *Zukunft*, Stuttgart, 1969; J. Moltmann, *Theology of Hope. On the Ground and the Implications of a Christian Eschatology*, London, 1967; W. Pannenberg, 'Eschatologie und Sinnerfahrung', in K. Krenn (ed.), *Die wirkliche Wirklichkeit Gottes. Gott in der Sprache heutiger Probleme*, Munich, 1974, pp. 143–58; K. Rahner, *Zur Theologie der Zukunft*, Munich, 1971. (This book consists of a number of essays selected from volumes of the author's *Schriften*); D. Wiederkehr, *Perspektiven der Eschatologie* (see ch. 3 note 10), esp. pp. 267–86.

CHAPTER 6

The political dimension of salvation

1   Cf. H. Peukert (ed.), *Diskussion zur „politischen Theologie"*, Mainz, 1969; W.-D. Marsch, *Gegenwart Christi in der Gesellschaft*, Munich, 1965, 'Faith and the World of Politics', in *Concilium*, vol. 6, no. 4 (June 1968); E. Feil and R. Weth (edd.), *'Diskussion zur „Theologie der Revolution"'* Munich, 1969².

2   Cf. J. B. Metz, ' "Politische Theologie" in der Diskussion', in H. Peukert (ed.), op. cit. (note 1), pp. 267–301; J. Möller, '„Befreiung von Entfremdung" als Kritik am christlichen Erlösungsglauben', in L. Scheffczyk (ed.), op. cit. (ch. 1 note 2), pp. 102–19; J. Moltmann, 'Theologische Kritik der politischen Religion', in J. B. Metz, J. Moltmann and W. Oelmüller,

Kirche in Prozeß der Aufklärung. Aspekte einer neuen "politischen Theologie", Munich, 1970, pp. 11–51; D. Sölle, *Political Theology*, Philadelphia, 1974.

[3] Cf. A. Ganoczy, *Sprechen von Gott in heutiger Gesellschaft. Weiterentwicklung der "Politischen Theologie"*, Freiburg im Breisgau, 1974; R. Höri (ed.), *Die Politik und das Heil*, Mainz, 1968; J. B. Metz, 'Erlösung und Emanzipation', in L. Scheffczyk, op. cit. (ch. 1 note 2), pp. 120–40.

[4] Advocates of critical theory have provided decisive stimulus to the consideration of this problem. Cf. J. Habermas, *Theorie und Praxis*, Frankfurt am Main, 1972². Among theological expositions we may mention: F. van den Oudenrijn, *Kritische Theologie als Kritik der Theologie. Theorie und Praxis bei Karl Marx—Herausforderung der Theologie*, Munich, 1972; F. Schupp, *Auf dem Weg zu einer kritischen Theologie* (Quaest. Disp. 64), Freiburg im Breisgau, 1974.

[5] Cf. G. Gutierrez, *A Theology of Liberation*, London, 1974, esp. pp. 3–19: 'Theology: A Critical Reflection'.

[6] Cf. H. Gollwitzer, 'Die gesellschaftlichen Implikationen des Evangeliums', in K. Herbert (ed.), *Christliche Freiheit im Dienst am Menschen*, Frankfurt am Main, 1972, pp. 141–52; H. Kessler, *Erlösung als Befreiung*, Düsseldorf, 1972, esp. pp. 61–95; W. Post, 'Jesus in der Sicht des modernen Atheismus, Humanismus und Marxismus', in F. J. Schierse (ed.), *Jesus von Nazareth*, Mainz, 1972, pp. 73–96.

[7] Cf. J. Moltmann, 'Existenzgeschichte und Weltgeschichte. Auf dem Wege zu einer politischen Hermeneutik des Evangeliums', in *Perspektiven der Theologie*, Munich, 1968, pp. 128–46. (This essay is one not included in the ET of this work: *Hope and Planning*, New York and London, 1971.) Id., *The Crucified God*, London, 1974, esp. pp. 317–40: 'Ways Towards the Political Liberation of Man'.

[8] H. Kessler, *Erlösung als Befreiung*, Düsseldorf, 1972, pp. 95–127. Cf. M. Horkheimer, *Die Sehnsucht nach dem ganz Anderen*, Hamburg, 1970.

[9] Cf. L. Dullaart, *Kirche und Ekklesiologie. Die Institutionslehre Arnold Gehlens als Frage an den Kirchenbegriff in der gegenwärtigen systematischen Theologie*, Munich, 1975; H. Gollwitzer, *Vortrupp des Lebens*, Munich, 1975; J. B. Metz, J. Moltmann and W. Oelmüller, op. cit. (note 2); J. Moltmann, 'The "Rose in the Cross of the Present": Towards an Understanding of the Church in Modern Society', in *Hope and Planning*, New York and London, 1971, pp. 130–54, *Theology and Joy*, New York and London, 1973, *The Church in the power of the Spirit: a contribution to messianic ecclesiology*, New York, 1977; K. Rahner, 'The function of the church as a critic of society', *Theol. Investig.* XIII, New York and London, 1974, pp. 229–49, *Strukturwandel der Kirche als Aufgabe und Chance*, Freiburg im Breisgau, 1972. Practical consequences for the Church's officers (ministers,

preachers, etc.) are drawn by Y. Spiegel and U. Teichler, *Theologie und gesellschaftliche Praxis*, Munich, 1974.

10 This section draws on L. Rütti, *Zur Theologie der Mission. Kritische Analysen und neue Orientierungen*, Munich, 1972. Cf. further J. Schmitz (ed.), *Das Ende der Exportreligion. Perspektiven einer künftigen Mission*, Düsseldorf, 1971; W. Kasper, 'Warum noch Mission?', in *Glaube und Geschichte*, Mainz, 1970, pp. 259–74; J. Baumgartner, *Vermittlung zwischenkirchlicher Gemeinschaft 50 Jahre Missionsgesellschaft Bethlehem Immensee*, Schöneck-Beckenried, 1971, esp. pp. 233–448: 'Missionstheorie und Geschichte'.

CHAPTER 7

Salvation in the present and future:
soteriology and eschatology

1 Cf. H. Rolfes (ed.), *Marxismus-Christentum*, Mainz, 1974; W.-D. Marsch, *Zukunft*, Stuttgart, 1969; R. Garaudy, J. B. Metz and K. Rahner, *Der Dialog. Oder: ändert sich das Verhältnis zwischen Katholizismus und Marxismus*, Reinbek bei Hamburg, 1966.

2 Cf. G. Greshake and G. Lohfink, *Naherwartung-Auferstehung-Unsterblichkeit. Untersuchungen zur christlichen Eschatologie* (Quaest. Disp. 71), Freiburg im Breisgau, 1975; J. Moltmann, *Umkehr zur Zukunft*, Munich, 1970, esp. pp. 148–67: 'Argumente für eine eschatologische Theologie'; W. Pannenberg, 'Weltgeschichte und Heilsgeschichte', in H. W. Wolff (ed.), *Probleme biblischer Theologie. Festschrift für Gerhard von Rad*, Munich, 1971, pp. 349–66; D. Wiederkehr, *Perspektiven der Eschatologie*, Einsiedeln, 1974, esp. pp. 267–86: 'Individuelle und solidarische Hoffnung'.

3 Cf. W. Heinen and J. Schreiner (edd.), *Erwartung-Verheißung-Erfüllung*, Würzburg, 1969; W. Kasper, 'Politische Utopie und christliche Hoffnung', in *Glaube und Geschichte*, Mainz, 1970, pp. 144–58; J. Moltmann, 'Hope and Planning', in *Hope and Planning*, New York and London, 1971, pp. 178–99; K. Rahner, *Zur Theologie der Zukunft* (see ch. 5 note 7), 'On the theology of revolution', in *Theol. Investig.* XIV/3, New York and London, 1976, pp. 314–30; G. Sauter, *Zukunft und Verheißung. Das Problem der Zukunft in der gegenwärtigen theologischen und philosophischen Diskussion*, Zurich, 1965.

4 Cf. I. Fetscher and M. Machoveč (edd.), *Marxisten und die Sache Jesu*, Munich, 1974; V. Gardavsky, *Gott ist nicht ganz tot*, Munich, 1968; J. M. Lochman, *Christus oder Prometheus? Die Kernfrage des christlich-marxistischen Dialogs und die Christologie*, Hamburg, 1972, *Marx begegnen. Was Christen und Marxisten eint und trennt*, Gütersloh, 1975.

5 M. Machoveč, *A Marxist Looks at Jesus*, London, 1976. For the non-

theistic interpretation of biblical symbols (e.g. the Kingdom of God), cf. D. Sölle, *Christ the Representative* (see ch. 1 note 4). Cf. also the discussion in D. Wiederkehr, 'Konfrontationen und Integrationen der Christologie', in *Theologische Berichte* II, Einsiedeln, 1973, pp. 11–119, esp. 99–118.

6   Cf. E. Bloch, *Das Prinzip Hoffnung*, Frankfurt am Main, 1973, esp. pp. 1392–1550, *Atheismus im Christentum* (see ch. 2 note 4), *Religion im Erbe*, Munich, 1967. The eschatological tradition in Christian piety and the Church's history is outlined by W. Nigg, *Das Ewige Reich. Geschichte einer Hoffnung*, Zurich, 1954[2].

7   K. Farner, 'Jesus als Brandstifter—Christus als Brandlöscher. Versuch einer provozierenden Skizze', in I. Fetscher and M. Machoveč (edd.), op. cit (see note 4), pp. 62–6.

8   Cf. H. Gollwitzer, *Die marxistische Religionskritik und der christliche Glaube*, Munich, 1967; A. Jäger, *Reich ohne Gott. Zur Eschatologie Ernst Blochs*, Zurich, 1969; J. M. Lochmann, *Trägt oder trügt die christliche Hoffnung? Biblisches Erbe in den Herausforderungen der Zeit*, Zurich, 1974; W.-D. Marsch, *Hoffen worauf? Auseinandersetzung mit Ernst Bloch*, Hamburg, 1963; J. Moltmann, *Theologie der Hoffnung*, Munich, 1966[5], esp. pp. 313–34: ' "Das Prinzip Hoffnung" und die "Theologie der Hoffnung". Ein Gespräch mit Ernst Bloch' (later than the ET of Moltmann's book), 'Die Kategorie Novum in der christlichen Theologie', in *Perspektiven der Theologie*, Munich, 1968, pp. 174–88 (see remark in ch. 6 note 7), *Im Gespräch mit Ernst Bloch. Eine theologische Wegbegleitung*, Munich, 1976; W. Pannenberg, 'The God of Hope', in *Basic Questions in Theology* II, London, 1971, pp. 234–49; J. Pieper, *Death and Immortality*, London, 1969; W. Zimmerli, *Der Mensch und seine Hoffnung im Alten Testament*, Göttingen, 1968, esp. pp. 163–78: 'Gespräch mit Ernst Bloch'.

CHAPTER 8

Present-day salvation praxis considered in relation to the origin and the completion of salvation

1   Most works on the relation between past and present redemption *presume* some theological mediation between history and the present, and the *problem* of that mediation is therefore not sufficiently adverted to. Cf. at least A. Darlap, 'Fundamentale Theologie der Heilsgeschichte', in *Mysterium Salutis* I. Einsiedeln, 1965, pp. 3–156 (French trans, I, 43–203); H. U. von Balthasar, *Theologie der Geschichte. Ein Grundriß*, Einsiedeln, 1950[2].

2   Cf. D. Sölle, *Christ the Representative* (see ch. 1 note 4), esp. pp. 107–12: 'The Provisionality of Christ'. The neglected problem of historical mediation is expressed in the one-sided emphasis on future at the expense of past redemption.

³ Cf. H. Kessler, *Erlösung als Befreiung*, Düsseldorf, 1972, esp. pp. 58–60. Kessler considers a selective understanding of redemption (incarnation or cross) as liable to misunderstand redemption as a once-for-all, closed salvific event, while the soteriological content of Jesus's whole life seems to the modern age more suitable for mediation. Cf. also W. Kasper, 'Grundlinien einer Theologie der Geschichte', in *Glaube und Geschichte*, Mainz, 1970, pp. 67–100; J. B. Metz, 'The Future in the Memory of Suffering', *Concilium* Vol. 6/8 (The God Question), June 1972, pp. 9–25; K. Rahner, 'The eternal significance of the humanity of Jesus for our relationship with God', *Theol. Investig.* III, Baltimore and London, 1967, pp. 35–46, 'Dogmatic questions on Easter', op. cit. IV, Baltimore and London, 1966, pp. 121–33, 'Christology within an evolutionary view of the world', op. cit. V, London, 1966, pp. 157–92, 'One mediator and many mediations', op. cit. VIII, New York and London, 1972, pp. 169–84; K. Rahner and W. Thüsing, *Christologie—systematisch und exegetisch* (Quest. Disp. 55), Freiburg im Breisgau, 1972, esp. pp. 35–50; D. Wiederkehr, 'Entwurf einer systematischen Christologie', in *Mysterium Salutis* III/1, Einsiedeln, 1970, pp. 477–645 (French trans. XI, 13–237), esp. 599–621.

⁴ Cf. H. Küng, *The Church*, New York and London, 1968; J. Moltmann, *The Church in the power of the Spirit* (see ch. 6 note 9); W. Pannenberg, *Theologie und Reich Gottes*, Gütersloh, 1971, esp. pp. 31–61: 'Reich Gottes und Kirche'; K. Rahner, 'The Church and the parousia of Christ', *Theol. Investig.* VI, Baltimore and London, 1969, pp. 295–312. On the significance of the eucharistic celebration, cf. A. Gerken, *Theologie der Eucharistie*, Munich, 1973.

⁵ H. Cox, *The Secular City*, London, 1966, *The Feast of Fools*, Cambridge, Mass., 1969; cf. G. M. Martin, *Fest und Alltag. Bausteine zu einer Theorie des Festes*, Stuttgart, 1973; J. Pieper, *Zustimmung zur Welt. Eine Theorie des Festes*, Munich, 1963.

⁶ Cf. H. U. von Balthasar, 'Der Unbekannte jenseits des Wortes', in *Spiritus Creator. Skizzen zur Theologie* III (see remark in ch. 7 note 3), Einsiedeln, 1967, pp. 95–105, 'Improvisation über Geist und Zukunft', ibid., pp. 123–55; C. Heitmann and H. Mühlen (edd.), *Erfahrung und Theologie des Heiligen Geistes*, Hamburg, 1974; W. Kasper, *Jesus der Christus*, Mainz, 1974, esp. pp. 296–300; W. Kasper and G. Sauter, *Kirche—Ort des Geistes*, Freiburg im Breisgau, 1976; H. Meyer et al., *Wiederentdeckung des Heiligen Geistes. Der Heilige Geist in der charismatischen Erfahrung und theologischen Reflexion*, Frankfurt am Main, 1974; J. Moltmann, *The Church in the power of the Spirit* (see ch. 6 note 9), notable for the mutual interpretation of ecclesiological and pneumatological mediations.

101

CONCLUSION

Soteriology as the preservation of faith's reality

1   Cf. G. Ebeling, 'Die Klage über das Erfahrungsdefizit in der Theologie als Frage nach ihrer Sache', in *Wort und Glaube* III (see remark in ch. 1 note 1), Tübingen, 1975, pp. 3–28; W. Pannenberg, *Theology and the Philosophy of Science*, Philadelphia and London, 1976, esp. pp. 297–345: 'Theology as the science of God'.

Index of Persons

Index of Subjects